"A groundbreaking book that will revolutionize your perception of 'God with us.' If you are ready to find hope-filled connection and freedom from loneliness, then *You Are Not Alone* is the book you have been looking for."

Mandy Arioto, president and CEO,
MOPS International

"*You Are Not Alone* presents help and hope to a generation starving for both."

Bill Crowder, vice president of ministry
content and cohost *Discover the Word*,
Our Daily Bread Ministries

"In this book, Elisa gives us practical ways to tend to the ache of loneliness. . . . Her words are a balm to the tired and restless heart."

Eryn Eddy, author and founder of
So Worth Loving

"With her signature transparency and approachable tone, Morgan offers biblical truths and practical applications that empower readers with hope. Her vulnerability and the testimonies of believers who have experienced God's mercy through bouts with loneliness establish a strong sense of camaraderie. Each of the six biblical affirmations create a solid foundation on which readers can stand with faith in the life-changing love, compassion, and power of our ever-present God."

Xochitl Dixon, author of *Waiting for God:
Trusting Daily in God's Plan and Pace*

"In *You Are Not Alone*, Elisa Morgan presents biblical wisdom for dealing with the pervasive, detrimental challenge of loneliness. I highly recommend this practical book that will help you find hope and freedom from loneliness in the presence and power of Christ."

Tom Felten, executive editor, *Our Daily Bread*

You Are Not Alone

SIX AFFIRMATIONS *from a* LOVING GOD

ELISA MORGAN

Our Daily Bread
Publishing™

Interior design by: Sherri L. Hoffman

Library of Congress Cataloging-in-Publication Data

Names: Morgan, Elisa, 1955- author.

Title: You are not alone : six affirmations from a loving God /
Elisa Morgan.

Description: Grand Rapids, MI : Our Daily Bread Publishing, [2021]
| Includes bibliographical references. | Summary: "Feelings of
loneliness can cause us to forget the truths of God's Word—that
He loves us, gives meaning to our lives, will never leave us. Be
encouraged, even in your darkest moments, by six affirming
reminders of our loving God's person, plan, presence, provision,
promise, and purpose"—Provided by publisher.

Identifiers: LCCN 2021019933 | ISBN 9781640701236 (paperback)

Subjects: LCSH: Loneliness—Religious aspects—Christianity. | God
(Christianity)—Love. | BISAC: RELIGION / Christian Living /
Inspirational

Classification: LCC BV4911 .M67 2021 | DDC 231/.6—dc23

LC record available at https://lccn.loc.gov/2021019933

Printed in the United States of America
22 23 24 25 26 27 28 / 8 7 6 5 4 3 2

To my Fabs:

J'Anne, Cindy, Debbie, and Carla.
You are not alone.
Thanks for always living out this reality.

Contents

Introduction

*Y*ou are not alone!

If you're like me, sometimes your response to this sentence is, "Really? Who's with me?"

You catalog the treasured few friends who honestly "get" you. They are present when you need to talk, they understand your struggles, and they do their best to respond to your needs. *You are not alone!*

You tick through work relationships, landing on the select colleagues who truly share your load. *You are not alone!*

You pause along your list of precious family members, remembering stages of life development as each transformed into who they are today, and you are so grateful for who you have become to each other. Spouse. Children and grandchildren. Parents. Siblings. Extended family. *You are not alone!*

No, you are not alone. There are lots of people with you.

But at times, it can seem like we're alone, can't it? That no one knows the real me and you, and therefore no one loves the real me and you. We might wonder just how impactful our lives have been. We can grow weary from carrying responsibilities alone. And at times we can feel dis-included from the meaning and joy that others seem to experience. People can let us down.

We know that the sentence, "You are not alone," ultimately means that despite disappointments with our human relationships, God is with us. And we can touch moment after moment when we've been utterly convinced that, indeed, He is. But to be honest, we can also struggle in seasons when we're less sure of His presence, and we actually wonder where He's gone. We know in our minds that God is constant. Yet in our experience, we can doubt.

But, hey! We desperately *want* to embrace God's 24-7 presence with us! We'd rather trust than doubt. Like the father of the demon-possessed boy in Mark 9:24, we whisper, "I do believe; help me overcome my unbelief." We long to wake up each morning completely convinced that we're not doing our days alone but rather that we're doing them with God. And we want to go to sleep at night with the peace that we are still not alone—that God embraces and holds our lives even as we rest.

Here's hope! In these pages, we'll walk through the multilayered experience of loneliness and pair up our struggles with the reality of what God offers in a relationship with himself. We'll look at what we can actually have in Him and how we can grab hold of everything He offers, even in the bleakest landscapes of life.

Every journey toward hope begins with embracing the reality of our need for it. So, in chapter 1, we'll look square in the face at "the pain of alone" and honestly see ourselves in the struggle. Then, we'll examine our six lonely struggles and pair them with six affirmations of the love God offers us in His Person. Each will build on the other until we emerge, hand in hand, with the hope God gives us in a life transformed from lonely to "unlonely."

You are not alone! Come along now . . . and let's discover the truth of this encouraging hope!

1

The Pain of Alone

"Lonely is in my joints and muscles.
It's in my head. It's in my genes."
—Michelle

*B*ack and forth. Back and forth. Back and forth. In my darkened bedroom, cocooned in my covers, my six-year-old self rocked in rhythm, searching for sleep. Our newly single-mom family had relocated thousands of miles from our former home. I had no idea when I'd see my father again. And now my new bedroom surrounded me with its strangeness. It didn't matter that my older sister slept just feet away in her own twin bed. Something in my being resisted the unknown of my changed life. Rocking seemed the only conduit to comfort, though I knew that in the morning my mother would curse over my tangled hair and struggle to free the strands before sending me off to school.

Before my parents' divorce, I don't remember being a lonely child. I was middle-born: two years after my sister and five years before my surprise younger brother. I'd felt loved and cared for and settled in my family place. And honestly, the "rocking" loneliness of adjusting to divorce eventually dissipated as I grew to find my footing. My heart refilled itself through make-believe play alongside my plastic horse collection, which I nuzzled underneath our azalea bush flowerbeds; through a newly discovered adoration of a black kitten I christened "Velvet;" and through biographies of brave women like Clara Barton, Florence Nightingale, and Liliuokalani checked out from my elementary school's bookmobile. (Remember those mobile libraries?)

"Lonely" first arrived through the divorce of my parents. Gradually, the feeling withdrew through the resilience of my personality and my ongoing choice of connection to pastimes and people. But throughout the years, "lonely" has reappeared at the door of my heart, sometimes shadowing over the corner of an afternoon, and in other seasons squatting uninvited over whole rooms in my being.

- During the beginnings of college, far, far away in an unknown state with a stranger as a roommate.
- With the reckoning realization that my father had somehow ranked his children by some scale of value, and I wasn't at the top.
- Living the self-supporting single life of a graduate student, wondering what would become of me.
- When everyone else became pregnant, and my husband and I waited and waited and waited for a child through adoption.
- As first my mother and then my father became terminally ill, and I flew to be with each of them as they passed, six years apart, leaving me an "orphan" from my mother at thirty-four, and from my father at forty.
- Once we adopted children and I was surely never

alone, surviving the long hours of mothering where the needs were unending; and I never seemed to have enough of me to go around.

- When my soul mate friend's husband was transferred twelve states away, and I was left forlorn. Then, decades later, when my walk-through-life friend contracted cancer.
- As my teenage children chose paths away from us, and we were left to pace the floor in prayer.
- Underneath the stunning betrayal of a trusted coworker.
- Separated from others by the call of leadership, where alone, I carried more than I could let on.
- Being dis-included from opportunities and roles I cherished.
- Enduring the "misses" in relationships where a parent, a friend, or a family member simply didn't "get" me, and I was left aching to be understood.
- Supporting friend after friend as their marriages ended in deep disappointment, shocking unfaithfulness, or undeniable depletion.
- Embracing the hollow hole of a grandbaby's passing while simultaneously struggling to support his grieving parents.
- Sitting alongside three friends in one year, crumpled and crumbled after the deaths of their husbands.
- Pouring myself out in tending to the needs of others while ignoring my own, resulting in an emptied-out heart and zero energy to continue.
- The sometimes-alone Christmas, Thanksgiving, Easter, birthday, Mother's Day, Whatever-Day celebrations.

Today, I ask myself, am I lonely? Now?

I quickly decide, "No, I'm not." My days are filled to over-full with writing and scheduling and recording and other creative efforts. Blank spots in my daily life quickly fill as I offer myself over to grandkids, to friends, and even to my dog, who is always delighted to take me on a walk at any time of the day or night.

But when I awaken in the night, chasing elusive sleep, my thoughts dig about and sometimes root down in a confusing conversation from the day before. I notice an unanswered email and feel ignored. I peer ahead at my to-dos and wish oh-so-much for someone else to share the load. I pick up the heavy burden of worry over thises and thats, and I wonder what God's up to if He's not fixing all the things that hurt my heart.

And "lonely" returns. The pain of "alone" sneaks back in. I feel not seen. Not heard. Not known. So, I conclude, not loved?

Lonely Me . . . Lonely You?

Do you relate? To the pain of alone? To the agony of lonely?

Perhaps "lonely" came early to you—as a child—as it did to me. You became acquainted and then gradually shifted "lonely" into a spot where you could keep it at bay. Away from your every moment.

Or "lonely" arrived in the aftermath of a crisis, when your job ended. When a child left. When you became single—again. When illness took up residence.

Or "lonely" seeped in between the door and the threshold of your life. Through the always-single singleness you never expected to be yours. In the world of retirement inside a pandemic when all the pastimes you'd planned were canceled. When your kids and grandkids began to juggle busy schedules that rarely included you in their days.

Depressed yet? Well, it IS depressing to face—really look at—the pain of alone in our lives, isn't it? Our thoughts and hearts drag downward like water draining from the sink.

> No one really loves me.
> No one knows the real me.
> My life has no meaning.
> I feel so alone.
> I'm tired of doing everything by myself.
> I feel rejected, not wanted.

Does it help to know you're not alone in your loneliness?

Our Lonely World

Loneliness is an epidemic today.

A recent survey found that almost half of all Americans feel alone. Nearly fifty percent feel lonely, left out, isolated from others, or lack companionship—saying their relationships lack meaning.[1] The number of "friends" people report having today is "one" or none. Twenty years ago, people could name, on average, four close connections.[2] Twenty-seven percent of survey respondents say they rarely or never feel there are people in their lives who understand them.[3] The loneliness epidemic strikes generationally; a British university found that loneliness is especially prevalent among those under twenty-five and over sixty-five.[4]

Add to this the reality that loneliness affects our health. Paul Irving, an expert on aging, says, "People with less meaningful connections experience disrupted sleep patterns, altered immune systems, and more inflammation and higher levels of stress. Experts suggest that loneliness can increase the risk of premature death by thirty percent, making it as risky as obesity."[5] Other research shows that the lack of close-knit, face-to-face relationships can be linked to high blood pressure, heart disease, stroke, and even cancer.[6] A health insurer's research suggests that loneliness has the same impact on mortality as smoking fifteen cigarettes a day![7]

All this is cause for serious concern!

Loneliness in Scripture

But hold on. We're not the first generation on this planet to experience the pain of alone. The Bible tells us about many lonely hearts—people crying out to God for comfort and care and intervention in their lonely world.

Hannah wailed out her loneliness before God in a desperate request for a child. Moses lived for forty years on the backside of a desert, tending his father-in-law's sheep and separated from all who knew his former, adopted-son-of-the-Egyptian-Pharaoh self. Ruth and her mother-in-law, Naomi, grieved in loneliness over the loss of their husbands and their way of life. And oh, the loneliness of stripped and laid-bare Job! Elijah experienced pits of depression and deep chasms of loneliness, believing he was the only faithful prophet left serving God. The weeping prophet, Jeremiah, held Israel's disobedience in his lonely heart. Paul endured years of persecution and imprisonment, separated from so many of his supporters.

Indeed, Scripture echoes with the wails of the lonely. And for surprisingly different reasons!

In Lamentations, a book composed of five poems of grief

over the demise of Jerusalem and the exile of Israel to Babylon, we see a great grief resulting in loneliness. The prophet Jeremiah uses the phrase "no one" five times in twenty-two verses, emphasizing the pain of alone.

How deserted lies the city,
once so full of people!
How like a widow is she,
who once was great among the nations!
She who was queen among the provinces
has now become a slave.
Bitterly she weeps at night,
tears are on her cheeks.
Among all her lovers
there is no one to comfort her;
All her friends have betrayed her;
they have become her enemies.
(Lamentations 1:1–2)

Multiple instances reveal that loneliness can result from not following God, as when Israel pulled away from God: "But your iniquities have separated you from God; your sins have hidden his face from you, so that he will not hear" (Isaiah 59:2).

Perhaps we see this most clearly in how loneliness came to David as a result of not following God. He struggled with sin and its painful consequences, and he expressed the pain of alone in psalm after psalm. Psalm 38 is a penitential psalm in which David acknowledges and confesses his sin and cries out from the physical, emotional, and social toll.

My heart pounds, my strength fails me;
even the light has gone from my eyes.

> My friends and companions avoid me
> because of my wounds;
> my neighbors stay far away.
> (Psalm 38:10–11)

And we see loneliness in Psalm 102, often attributed to David, where the subtitle ascribes the psalm to an afflicted person who has grown weak and pours out a penitential lament before the Lord: "I am like a desert owl, like an owl among the ruins. I lie awake; I have become like a bird alone on a roof" (Psalm 102:6–7).

In other moments, the pain of alone afflicts as a result of actually following God. David was anointed king of Israel, but he was not crowned for over a decade. He fought off opposition from Saul, and he served God as "a man after [his] own heart" (Acts 13:22). Psalm 25 shows that David suffered loneliness as a result of his obedience.

> Turn to me and be gracious to me,
> for I am lonely and afflicted.
> Relieve the troubles of my heart
> and free me from my anguish.
> Look on my affliction and my distress
> and take away all my sins.
> See how numerous are my enemies
> and how fiercely they hate me!
> (Psalm 25:16–19)

What might be most startling to realize is that Jesus himself experienced loneliness. In His days on earth, many deserted Him (John 6:66–67), His disciples left Him to pray alone in the garden of Gethsemane (Mark 14:32–42), and Peter denied Him (Mark 14:66–72). On the cross, Jesus suffered perhaps the greatest pain of alone as His Father turned His face away from the sin that Jesus carried for us. In His last moments on earth, the torment of alone burst forth from His lips as He cried out in a loud voice, "My God, my God, why have you forsaken me?" (Matthew 27:46).

Loneliness has haunted humankind since one climactic moment, revealed in the first several chapters of the Bible. Because it was "not good" (the concept conveyed is "not complete or whole") that humans be alone (Genesis 2:18), God created Adam and Eve. To be together. With Him. Alas, when the first humans disobeyed God's only command, not to eat of the tree of the knowledge of good and evil (Genesis 2:17), their union with their Creator was broken. The pain of alone entered, slicing open a hollow of hurt in their hearts—and ours as well.

Types of Loneliness

As a result, we face the pain of alone on many levels. Some of us experience certain aspects more than others. Some may suffer a checkmark in every box. Where does the pain of alone enter your days?

Emotional loneliness: No one really loves me. The feeling of being unloved.

Relational loneliness: No one knows the real me. The experience of being unknown, or "missed," or doing life without relationship.

Vocational loneliness: My life has no meaning. The concern of having little defined purpose in life.

Spiritual loneliness: I feel so alone. The experience of being cut off from God.

Physical loneliness: No one is around to share the load. The isolation of not having people to help.

Situational loneliness: I feel rejected, unwanted. The experience of not being included or desired in various life circumstances.

Hope: You Are Not Alone!

Someone has suggested that loneliness is ultimately a kind of "homesickness" for God. The remedy for the pain of alone comes from embracing hope in three understandings.

First, we were never meant to be alone. When we realize we were made for companionship, we find our footing in the swirl of lonely. We're not weird or wrong or somehow depraved for feeling lonely. Lonely is how we were created to feel when we are unhinged from connection.

Second, God offers a solution for the pain of alone by inviting us into relationship with himself and others. Even when our ancestral parents strayed from God, He continued to craft a solution by drawing them back to himself. He allowed them to sense their great separation from Him and therefore their great need to be reunited. He does the same with each of us.

And third, God reminds us of His ongoing offering in our loneliness. He tenderly bends to hear our hurts and answers with affirmations from His heart.

When we cry, "No one really loves me," He *promises*: "I will always love you."

When we struggle, "No one knows the real me," He responds with an unmatched *perception* of who we are: "I know you because I made you."

When we worry, "My life has no meaning," He underlines our *purpose*: "I know the plans I have for you."

When we mourn, "I feel so alone," He offers His *presence*: "I will not leave you alone; I will be with you."

When we sigh, "I'm tired of doing everything alone," He gives *provision*: "I will provide for you."

When we confess, "I feel rejected and not wanted," He presents *perspective*: "I will use all things for your good and My glory."

God offers six affirmations in the various pains of our alone:

His promise
His perception
His purpose
His presence
His provision
His perspective

Simple, huh? But not simplistic. Instead, just the opposite. Coming to grips with our experiences of loneliness requires us to face the pain of alone. And being released from the disorienting grip of loneliness on our hearts happens as we respond to our beckoning God, who woos us toward the solution He put in place long ago and applies continuously in our lives today.

You are not alone. Come along with me, and let's find out why.

2

God's Promise

*"I know I am deeply loved—by God,
family, and friends; even my boss loves me.
But, . . . it isn't enough sometimes!"*
—Bess

Our Struggle: No one really loves me.
God's Affirmation: I will always love you.

*W*e met in a park and sat across from each other on the benches of a one-piece metal table unit, its legs firmly anchored to the concrete beneath our feet. While her words poured out freely, my friend's heart seemed as locked down as our picnic place.

"I just wish—oh, how I wish—I could feel completely, truly, really loved at some point before I die. And before you say it—I know you love me, but *you* are not enough."

My own tongue tied up. I had nothing to say in response. I'd known this friend's heart for decades. I'd tried to "be there" in both dark and bright moments. In many ways, my husband and I had truly been *family* for her. Yet her confessed desire rang true, and I knew better than to deny the utter loneliness she expressed.

So, I began to pray that she would, indeed, experience what it is like to be "completely, truly, really loved" before she dies. I've journaled my requests on her behalf along with her small stutter steps of faith that might one day chart progress. So far, it's been three years since I began praying this way, with little observable results. If anything, this loved one is even more alone because of new health and financial challenges.

Emotional Loneliness

Oh, the ache!

The pain of alone crescendos in the emotional realm. Emotional loneliness arises from feeling a lack of relationships or attachment.[1] Often it expresses itself in "chronic loneliness" that endures longer than a day or a night, accompanied by symptoms like negative thinking, the inability to connect with others, exhaustion, and feelings of isolation—sometimes even when others are around.[2]

How do these lonely emotions grow so strong in us?

Our families of origin form our lonely feelings.

Emotional loneliness can develop from growing up in a dysfunctional family where love is meted out only after correct behavior, where offspring are ranked in value by gender or birth order, where parents are emotionally or physically absent from their children, or where other forms of abuse occur. We might be able to identify this kind of loneliness when as a child, we were left alone too much, when we latchkeyed ourselves to and from school, or when we were forced into "adulting" in order to care for a parent who couldn't care for us. For some of us, identifying a childhood cause of our adult loneliness may not come until we are well into our mature years and often only with the help of counseling.

When I was five, my father called me into his home office and onto his lap. He turned me to look into his eyes, and he told me, "I've decided I don't love your mother anymore. We're getting a divorce." Soon my new family of a single mom, older sister, younger brother, and me moved across the country, and my rocking myself to sleep at bedtime began. I saw my father only once or twice a year when he and his new wife came to take my older sister and me out to dinner (leaving my baby brother at home with my depressed mother to develop his own "emotional lonely"). We were just children, but we worked hard to enter the adult conversation around us in order to be noticed and fit in. Still, I felt odd and not wanted.

It took years for me to understand that the holes in my lonely heart had come from the ripping apart of my family.

Is this your story too? Or something similar? The emotional lonely of childhood hits us in a time when we simply don't have the tools to understand it—much less process it. Instead, we come to child-sized conclusions that there must be something wrong with us. That no one ever really loved us.

Our growing up years form our lonely feelings.

The emotion of loneliness might appear later for some of us—perhaps in the middle school years of not belonging to certain cliques or "in crowds." Or it could be in experiencing the victimization of bullying, or social rejection, or just being different from the norm around us.

In middle school, my days began with the blaring sound of my mother's alarm going off in our ranch-style house in Houston, Texas. It was my job to wake her each morning and get her off to work because, well, we were a single-mom family and we needed our mom to work. And because my mother struggled with alcohol, she couldn't get herself up and off to her job.

We were pretty much the only divorced family in our neighborhood in those days. In an upper middle-class development where my friends lived in two-parent, seemingly stable homes with the dad in a career and the mom at home, I felt different—and ashamed. Rather than inviting friends from school to my messy house, I'd either suggest we meet at a park or finagle an invitation to their house. But often I simply made an excuse and retreated to my room where I could close the door and be somewhat safe.

Today around twenty-three percent of children under the age of eighteen live in a single-parent household.[3] The numbers have grown, and single parents are less of an oddity. Does that make it "easier" for tweens and teens to "fit in?" Who knows? A myriad of other challenges appears in these developmental years, including peer pressure, economic stress, social media comparison, and bullying—all leading to an undeniable emotional loneliness.

Our adult realities form our lonely feelings.

As we age, emotional loneliness continues. A dear friend passes away, and we are left without that special person who truly understood. A job ends, and our identified reason to get up in the morning evaporates with it, along with our financial security. Even when we enjoy a boisterous family and meaningful friendships and work, we can feel lonely in the midst of all we're doing. Somehow missed. Taken for granted. Unseen.

There are those who spend years, decades, or even all their adult lives as singles in a world of couples. Whether never-married, divorced, or widowed, singles can find themselves perpetually in search of a "plus one" in order to be included in events. They can be left on their own for holidays or left out of the church "family" made up of marrieds with children.

Bess shares, "I'm sixty-six, single, a mother of two sons (who are exceptionally devoted and attentive but not perfect). I work full time with a large bank, have strong family and friend relationships. I know I am deeply loved—by God, family, and friends; even my boss loves me. But . . . it isn't enough sometimes! I have never experienced the cherished, valued affection from a man. I talk with God about this regularly and confess guilt since maybe He thinks, 'Look, Girl, I have given you so much!' I don't like to focus on it, but there is a hole in my heart because of it."

And in the advanced seasons of life, when our busyness downshifts, our budgets tighten, and our living quarters shrink, the feeling of loneliness can sting with a bitter pain that refuses to be soothed.

Oh-so-many of us long to *really be loved*. Before we die. When we don't feel we are really loved, we experience the pain of alone that is emotional loneliness.

Emotional Loneliness in Scripture

We are not alone. The Psalms include many expressions of loneliness—especially expressions of emotional loneliness where feelings are felt and poured out in vivid words. Bill Crowder, my cohost on *Discover the Word*, a radio program and podcast from Our Daily Bread Ministries, offers a great perspective on the emotions of the Psalms. "I think back to when I was in seminary, and I took a class on the exposition of Psalms. On the first day of class the professor made a statement about the book of Psalms being an inspired collection of human emotional reactions to life." Makes good sense, doesn't it?

In his psalms, David seems to have been a man who felt all the "feels." Psalm 22 was perhaps written when he was fleeing from a mentally unstable Saul.

Read the first twenty-one verses . . . and if you're comfortable doing so, take a highlighter or pen and underline all the phrases that describe David's emotional loneliness.

My God, my God, why have you forsaken me?
Why are you so far from saving me,
so far from my cries of anguish?
My God, I cry out by day, but you do not answer,
by night, but I find no rest.

Yet you are enthroned as the Holy One;
you are the one Israel praises.
In you our ancestors put their trust;
they trusted and you delivered them.
To you they cried out and were saved;
in you they trusted and were not put to shame.

But I am a worm and not a man,
scorned by everyone, despised by the people.
All who see me mock me;
they hurl insults, shaking their heads.
"He trusts in the LORD," they say,
"let the LORD rescue him.
Let him deliver him,
since he delights in him."

Yet you brought me out of the womb;
you made me trust in you, even at my mother's breast.
From birth I was cast on you;
from my mother's womb you have been my God.

Do not be far from me,
for trouble is near
and there is no one to help.

Many bulls surround me;
strong bulls of Bashan encircle me.
Roaring lions that tear their prey
open their mouths wide against me.
I am poured out like water,
and all my bones are out of joint.
My heart has turned to wax;
it has melted within me.
My mouth is dried up like a potsherd,
and my tongue sticks to the roof of my mouth;
you lay me in the dust of death.

Dogs surround me,
a pack of villains encircles me;
they pierce my hands and my feet.
All my bones are on display;
people stare and gloat over me.
They divide my clothes among them
and cast lots for my garment.

But you, LORD, do not be far from me.
You are my strength; come quickly to help me.
Deliver me from the sword,
my precious life from the power of the dogs.
Rescue me from the mouth of the lions;
save me from the horns of the wild oxen.

The phrases are powerful, aren't they? In many instances,
the wording is so vulnerable, so painful, that it might make

us cringe in discomfort. Turn away. Many commentators suggest that the Holy Spirit actually spoke about the crucifixion of Jesus through David in this psalm. Doesn't that magnify further the suffering expressed? "Why have you forsaken me?" (v. 1). "I am a worm and not a man . . . scorned . . . despised" (v. 6). "Roaring lions . . . open their mouths wide against me" (v. 13). "I'm poured out like water . . . my heart has turned to wax" (v. 14). "You lay me in the dust of death" (v. 15). "Dogs surround me" (v. 16).

Now go back and read the passage again, this time using a different color to underline how—in the middle of his emotional loneliness—David calls on God for help. David reminds himself of God's sovereignty (vv. 3–5), of God's hand in creating and sustaining him (vv. 9–11) and of God's ability to rescue him (vv. 19–21).

David expresses feelings—strong feelings of emotional loneliness—followed by faithful utterances and choices to trust.

Emotions and Our Faith

We might brake here—even skid to a stop. Right? Sure, God likely loves it when we choose faith and trust. But is it okay to express emotions—strong negative feelings of sadness, anger, frustration, envy—loneliness?

Yes, it is.

In fact, the Bible shows us that even Jesus, fully God and fully human in every way, dared to *feel* before His Father. In the garden of Gethsemane, the night before He went to the cross, Jesus prayed three times for the cup of suffering to be removed. Matthew 26:37–38 tells us Jesus was "sorrowful and troubled . . . overwhelmed with sorrow to the point of death." He begged His disciples to stay awake and pray with Him.

Instead, they slept. And in the utter loneliness of His night alone, God provided companionship for Jesus as "an angel from heaven appeared to him and strengthened him" (Luke 22:43). Even after such solace, Jesus was still "in anguish, . . . his sweat was like drops of blood falling to the ground" (v. 44).

Jesus, the Son of God, experienced and expressed the pain of alone before His Father. Fully. Freely. Honestly.

But He also yielded in faith and trust to His Father's ways by confessing, "Yet not my will, but yours be done" (Luke 22:42).

Feelings, whether negative or "processed," are not wrong. Even Jesus felt feelings. Feelings inform us. Like an indicator on a car's dashboard, they let us know what's going on within. Coupled with faith, feelings reveal our human need and can, if we pay attention, lead us to hope.

How can we combine this practice of fully and freely expressing our feelings with choosing faith and trust in our good God in our own emotional loneliness?

Moving from Living Lonely to Living Loved

When I was a child, around eight or nine years old, each Sunday morning my mother dropped my sister and me off at a neighborhood church and then returned for us several hours later. We didn't really know what to do with ourselves, so we joined the adult choir (they were very patient people!), attended the worship service, and then finished up the time in Sunday school. Early in my life, I came to love Jesus. I remember locking eyes with a painting of Jesus at the far end of a long hall and daring myself not to break the stare until I arrived, with a bit of a lump in my throat before the image. His kind and patient eyes seemed to see all the way down into my elementary-age heart with a powerful kind of knowing.

As a teen, I found out that there was even more to God than I'd been taught. I could actually have a relationship with Him. I could know Him and I could—What?! Be loved by Him!

At first, this discovery hit me as a bit *Blah, blah, blah. Big deal.* God loves me. Jesus loves me. It was just a fact. Sentences in songs. But gradually, God began to woo me closer into an understanding I never knew I needed. The lonely holes in my heart cracked open to reveal not just what had been denied me in my parents' lack of love. They also described my own love deficiency.

I was living unloved. Because I thought I had to. Because I'd decided that I didn't deserve to be loved. Because love was beyond me. And living unloved as I was, I was living separated from God. Apart from Him.

It took a while for me to absorb that so much of my lonely could be changed. That my lonely was not just a result of what had been done or not done to me by my parents. There was another layer of lonely within me that resulted from my choice to live separated from God. Could I be protecting myself from further disappointment? Gradually, I learned something vital from friends who lived a bit farther down the road in their faith than I did. I learned that because God had poured out His love for me in the extravagant gift of Jesus's death on a cross, I would never have to live separated from Him—from love—ever again.

I remember my face reddening as I realized that for all of my life up to this point, I had pretty much taken God for granted. Of course He loved me! God is love. But this new-found, tremendous kind of love slayed me. I felt embarrassed that I'd missed the point. Eagerly, I confessed my mistake and hungrily invited Him closer.

Something in me shifted. I didn't want to live lonely anymore. I wanted to live loved.

"My God, my God, why have you forsaken me?" Like David in Psalm 22:1, our feelings of emotional loneliness can be so strong that we conclude God has abandoned us. *No one really loves me!* But God has not left us. He is closer than we can ever imagine. How do we know this? Because the reality is this: When Jesus cried, "My God, my God, why have you forsaken me?" (Matthew 27:46) as He hung from the cross in *all* the pain of *all* our alone, enduring the ultimate emotional loneliness of separation from His Father because of our sin, He did it so you and I would never have to be separated from Him again. Oh, we will surely feel the pain of alone in this life. But we will truly not be alone in that pain. And it is not the only emotion we will feel.

I Will Always Love You

I joined a Bible study where a teacher assigned us to read the book of Romans. As a teen, Romans was heady—even scary—material. "For all have sinned and fall short of the glory of God" (3:23). We are "justified by faith" (3:28). We are "dead to sin but alive to God" (6:11). Important, yet to my young mind, confusing teachings.

And then I came to chapter eight. It's about how the Holy Spirit helps us as believers in Jesus as we live in this world. I discovered the breakthrough crescendo in verses 31–39: that there isn't anything in all creation that can separate—create distance or a space between—us from the love of God.

There isn't *anything.*

Any. Thing.

We are *inseparable* from God's love. God's love is *inseparable* from us.

To help explain "why" we can't be separated from God's love, in Romans 8 Paul asks a series of questions and then answers them.

- If God is for us, who can be against us? *No one!* (v. 31)

- He who did not spare His own Son, but gave Him up for us all—how will He not also, along with Him, graciously give us all things? *He has!* (v. 32)

- Who will bring any charge against those God has chosen? *No one!* (v. 33)

- Who then is the one who condemns? *No one!* (v. 34)

In verse 34, Paul provides the answer to the biggest question before he even asks it: "Christ Jesus who died—more than that, who was raised to life—is at the right hand of God and is also interceding for us."

Then comes his big question—the one he's already answered. "Who shall separate us from the love of Christ?" (v. 35)

Answer: *There isn't ANY THING!*

To underline and illustrate this stunning truth, Paul composed a long list of the "any things" that can't separate us from God's love. Later in life, as I studied more deeply, I discovered that the "any things" Paul wrote about are actually things he had personally experienced. His letters to the first-century church (especially 2 Corinthians 10–11) reveal that he had personally endured these "any things" and had survived—still attached to God's love, and God's love was still present with him.

So, I tried an experiment for myself. One at a time, I took each "any thing" and asked God to show me how even that very experience, trial, or struggle could never separate me from His love. To be honest, I can't remember exactly how each played out in my adolescent days. What I do remember is that each "any thing" was answered with a "Nope, not that!"

From time to time, I've reentered this "inseparable" exercise and in each application, I've never discovered an exception. There hasn't been any thing in my past and there isn't any thing in my present and there won't be any thing in my future that can separate me from the love of God in Christ Jesus.

PRACTICE
Inseparable—What Are Your "Any Things"?

So, now it's time to create your own "inseparable" exercise. What are your "any things"?

Take each "any thing" in Paul's Romans 8 list and ask God to show you how that thing can't separate you from His love. One a day. One a week. One a month. However God leads. Wade in and watch God demonstrate His love for you. You might journal your findings, so when you've completed the list you have proof to remind yourself of this amazing reality.

Below you'll find each "any thing" with its meaning as

Paul included it in his list of any things, as well as examples. May these illustrations open your heart to your own any things! There isn't any thing that can separate you from the love of God in Christ Jesus!

Trouble: a general term for stress (Romans 8:35)

Paul uses the word "trouble" some twenty-one times in his writings. It refers to the ongoing, nearly ever-present struggle of living. Read 2 Corinthians 1:8–10. What troubles does Paul mention he has endured? How does he underline that those troubles didn't separate him from the love of God?

Sample "troubles" could include family, marital and relational struggles, unemployment or stress at work, health issues, financial needs, daily stresses, and pains.

Name the specific trouble you are experiencing that can't separate you from the love of God.

Hardship: a state of being "squeezed" by outward affliction that causes internal pressure (Romans 8:35)

In the English language, the word *hardship* is used in various ways.

Hardship clause: in a contract where an unforeseen event makes it impossible for one part to fulfill an agreement.

Hardship post: When a United States diplomat is placed in a position where risky conditions exist, including such things as a dangerous climate, high crime, poor healthcare, or pollution.

Undue *hardship*: When a business is excused from providing certain benefits when it might put them out of business to do so.

These phrases may help you identify how the concept of "hardship" is present in your life.

Paul wrote about his own "thorn in the flesh" in 2 Corinthians 12:7–10 and how God not only had allowed it but also revealed His power in Paul's weakness through it.

Name the specific hardship in your life right now that can't separate you from the love of God.

Persecution: To be harassed or oppressed by a systematic effort, rejected for faith (Romans 8:35)

Perhaps you've experienced persecution for your faith as Paul did. Read 1 Corinthians 4:8–13 to familiarize yourself with all he went through.

If you haven't experienced such a struggle, perhaps you can identify other kinds of oppression or harassment in your life. Of race? Of gender? Of status? Of education?

List the persecution that can't separate you from the love of God.

Famine: a state of hunger, or not having enough food (Romans 8:35)

In New Testament times, the food supply was definitely challenged. Famine was not unusual. We may live in an age when famine is rarer, but we can all relate to periods or seasons when we've been hungry for food, and hungry for other things that sustain our lives.

Read 1 Corinthians 4:11 and 2 Corinthians 11:27 and note Paul's experience of famine. Now read Luke 4:1–4 and consider how Jesus endured hunger.

As you think through your experience with the great "lacks" that make you hunger, the famines in your days, how do you know they can't separate you from the love of God?

Nakedness: being unclothed, a range of undress (Romans 8:35)

As with famine, nakedness was not uncommon in the first century. Clothes were essential, yes. But clothing did not come in abundance. Most people had a single article, such as a tunic or a robe.

Paul's words from 1 Corinthians 4:11–12 and 2 Corinthians 11:27 apply here as they did to famine.

The concept Paul is pointing to is really the shame of being exposed.

Think through the layers of your life where shame points arrows at your greatest deficits. List several of these painful points and consider how, even in them, you cannot be separated from the love of God.

Danger: being at risk due to a state of threatening circumstances (Romans 8:35)

Paul wrote to the Corinthians to warn them of the great danger of false teachers who stressed that salvation came through obedience to the law rather than simply through embracing the grace of God's gift in Jesus. If anyone had suffered in obedience, it was Paul, as he cataloged in 2 Corinthians 11:24–28.

When have you been in danger? Perhaps physically, as Paul was? Or perhaps you've faced other kinds of danger such as the twisting of crazy teaching or the presence of toxic people in your life? How does God want you to know that even in these situations, you can't be separated from His love?

Sword: being threatened with your very life (Romans 8:35)

In the early church, Christians were persecuted and sometimes even martyred. They could be regarded as nothing more than animals to be butchered, often for entertainment purposes. Paul writes of his encounters with the "sword," or being threatened with his life. In 1 Corinthians 4:9 he references the execution of Christians by Rome, where the apostles were exposed to death, "like those condemned to die in the arena." He goes on in verse 11, reporting he was "brutally treated," which has the sense of being forcefully slapped in the face. In 2 Corinthians 11:23 he mentions that he was "exposed to death again and again."

The reality is that most of us will not face the sword in a literal fashion, though some may as in war or violence. Neither are God's people immune from suffering nor does suffering remove us from being God's people. Instead, as Paul goes on in Romans 8:37, "in all these things we are more than conquerors through him who loved us." The word *conquerors* has the idea of "continuing to conquer, over and over again." In other words, when we suffer—even under the threat of the sword—God makes us "overcomers."

In what area of your life is God telling you that you can continue to conquer suffering, over and over again, and that it can't separate you from His love?

Anything Else in All Creation: not *any* thing (Romans 8:38–39)

Remember taking cumulative tests in school? They measured learning that was accomplished over a period of time. For example, a cumulative final exam would cover material taught over an entire course, rather than just the last few weeks of a semester.

Paul's list of "any things" culminates in the last few verses, building on everything he's already covered. In Romans 8:38, Paul writes, "I am convinced," meaning he has absolute certainty that specific, all-encompassing realities cannot separate us from the love of God. He then creates a list of comparisons—four pairs and two stand-alones.

- Neither death nor life: Here Paul expresses the extremes of existence.
- Neither angels nor demons: Extremes of the spiritual world.
- Neither the present nor the future: Extremes of time.
- Neither height nor depth: Extremes of space.
- Any powers: Extremes of power.
- Anything else in all creation: Extremes in the entire created realm.

Wow! Think about each element and how experiences in your life validate that there isn't "any thing"—in any extreme—that can separate you from the love of God.

in place while Miss Hailey called roll, using first names only. She came to my name and projected, "Alissa."

"Here," I answered and then raised my hand, interrupting her before she could announce the next name. "Excuse me, Miss Hailey?" I asked.

"What is it?" she responded, pen poised over her clipboard.

"My name is Elisa—pronounced 'Aleeeeesa.' You pronounced it 'Alissa,' with a short i."

A moment passed while Miss Hailey considered my comment. Abruptly, she gathered her thoughts, squinted her eyes just a bit and quipped, "Well, you'll just have to get used to how I pronounce it. You're Alissa in here."

Though I held my face in place, inside, my heart fell. I felt unknown. True to her word, through all of fifth grade, I was "Alissa," not Elisa, to Miss Hailey.

Who knows your name? How to spell it? How to pronounce it? Who knows who you are behind its label? At the center of our relational loneliness—feeling alone without or even with relationships—is our need to be known.

Relational Loneliness

Relational loneliness grows when no one knows our name, how to spell it, how to pronounce it, and at the core, who we are behind its label. Even when we can name spouse, family, friends, and coworkers whose lives bump into our lives, we can still experience a kind of being "missed" and therefore, loneliness.

How does relational loneliness take root in our lives?
We think we're supposed to do life alone.

Today's individualism prescribes that we be strong and independent in order to be seen as successful. It's up to the individual to meet her goals and desires. Those who are "mature" will self-manage, independently and without much connection to others.

So, when we experience relational loneliness, without relationships where we are known, we conclude that we'd just better snap out of it. Buck up. Handle it. And down, down, down we stuff the yearning to connect. Some sociologists suggest a hyper-individualism[1] or "toxic individualization"[2] may result in the demise of society as we've known it.

We live in a world that prescribes isolation for our own safety.

The COVID-19 pandemic initiated a new level of isolation in our world. Social distancing, masking, Zoom meetings, travel prohibitions, postponed life celebrations, and general "stay away from each other" guidelines—all for our own safety—have resulted in an unparalleled relational loneliness. We've actually become afraid of relationships and connection.

We live and work in a fractured society.

One think tank suggests, "America's social fabric is being ripped to shreds by distrust, loneliness, alienation, inequality, racism, spiritual emptiness, and tribal enmity."[3] Polarized by our political stances, belief systems, and newsfeed preferences, social media schisms us further apart from others who might hold different views. That's a lot to overcome! We conclude it just might be better to "stay in our own lane" than risk connection where we might be misunderstood or even rejected.

While divorce rates have dropped in recent years, marriage rates have as well.[4] According to a Pew Research study, children today grow up in a variety of family situations, including two-parent first marriage (46 percent), two-parents remarried (15 percent), cohabiting (7 percent) and single parent (26 percent).[5] Our global workforce stations employees all around the world, uprooting family systems and friendships.

Perhaps this last cause is core to our relational loneliness: *We've swallowed the myth that we'll be surrounded by friends and families in such a way that we won't (ever) experience loneliness.*

And then life happens. We move. We change jobs. We empty out our nest. Our marriage breaks apart. Barna Institute notes that one-third of adults and practicing Christians say anxiety or depression (or both) have impacted their close relationships, making them the most common barriers to relational satisfaction.[6]

Kristine shares, "I have been divorced for almost two years after being in a difficult marriage for twenty years. I miss being married, and I feel so lonely when I see how difficult it is to date. I am overwhelmed at times with longing and the feeling like life will never be normal again. I also wonder how in the world I could ever meet anyone when all I do is go to work and church."

Do You Have a "Person"?

In a somewhat desperate attempt to create connection in our individualized, isolated, splintered, and broken society, we can buy into the myth that everyone has a "person." We just need to find that certain someone who will know us through and through, in a safe way. Then we won't be lonely. Right?

Years back, I remember the relationship forged between two friends on a TV medical drama. A female doctor struggled to find her way through the complex and highly competitive workings of her hospital training program. When asked to put down a contact on her emergency form, she identified a coworker who had seemed to have her back in all matters—both in work and life. As the show went on, these two characters routinely referred to one another as each other's "person." Their label became a trend, leading to over a million posts using #myperson.[7]

Being someone's person, or having a person, might be platonic as in the "bosom friend" designation from *Anne of Green Gables,* or it might become romantic as in the "you-complete-me" moniker of the movie *Jerry Maguire.* Bottom line, this kind of person is a soul mate. Someone who knows you so well that they finish your sentences, order for you exactly what you would have ordered, show up at the very moment they're needed without being asked and who—no matter what—are *always* willing to do life with you.

Do you have a person?

Most of us would respond, "Sorta." There's the best friend from high school who remembers us from who we were as "bubbly" or "bookish" or "blonde." The young mom friend who walks beside us through pregnancy and late nights and diapers and the extra twenty pounds and the marriage upheavals. The coworker who covers when we're carpooling and brings us a latte on a particularly stressful morning. The spouse who rubs our feet or does the dishes or shares the remote.

Most of us sorta have a person. Until we don't. When he or she zones us out and tunes into the game instead. Or responds to our "What do you want to do this weekend?" with their own, "I don't know, what do you want to do?" and then never plans anything to do at all. Or commits to our kid's birthday party and at the last minute doesn't show.

Or gives us a pumpkin spice candle for our birthday when we've been extremely clear—even joked together—that we can't stand pumpkin spice anything. How could they have forgotten?

That's when we realize the person we thought was our "person" isn't. We feel missed, overlooked, and not known.

Tricia writes about her relational loneliness. "I have been struggling with the loneliness feeling for the past six years or so. I love to stay busy and be around people. It's a shock to me when I am in a group setting with people I love and like, and this feeling of loneliness sweeps over me. I sit and think they really do not know me deep down. They should, but I am not convinced they do. I make an early departure and no one can understand why, since I am often the person who organized the gathering! I feel lonely with my spouse and son as well. Do they really know me? If so, would they know my favorite song, flower, or book? It baffles me that often the people I spend the most time with create a loneliness in my soul."

Some have a person until they lose that special someone due to the breakup of a relationship—or a divorce. My sweet friend and cohost of the *God Hears Her* podcast, Eryn Eddy, was married for nine years before experiencing the amputation of divorce. Looking back, Eryn comments, "I was in a relationship for a very long time. And I felt lonely." At times, Eryn can feel alone as a newly single woman as well.

Then there's the ultimate loss of our person through death. The one we'd covenanted to live life with until death parts us is suddenly gone. Karen, Tracey, and Cheryl are three dear friends—all of whom became widows within the same eighteen-month period. And all of them were either under or just over the fifty-year-old mark. Too young!

I've watched and wept alongside them as they've learned to navigate single parenting, solo work, and the long look ahead to the rest of their lives. Aloneness is their constant companion. It stands so starkly against the once-full-to-overflowing life of marriage.

Death steals more than spouse persons. Kim describes her loneliness when her father passed: "When the world was thrust into COVID-19 quarantine, my father was already an eight-year resident of a very nice and loving Alzheimer's facility. I went from seeing him two to three times a week to not seeing him at all. . . . I was able to see my dad through Facetime, but because of his progression of Alzheimer's it was hard for him to focus or even understand what was going on. I missed him immensely. My caring for him, touching him, and feeding him was reduced to a small video screen. I was still very grateful for that, but I became very sad. Daddy began to deteriorate. He just didn't look the same. He couldn't figure it all out, but we were still very excited and grateful just to see him. Then he was diagnosed with COVID-19. Suddenly he began to slowly succumb to pneumonia, and then COVID. I lost my precious daddy, a Vietnam veteran, ordained deacon, and a father of nine adult children. My solace is that he was saved, sanctified, and living his life for Christ's gain. Today I'm married and a co-pastor—but I am still lonely for my earthly daddy."

Then there are those among us who feel as if we've never really had a "person." Like Bess, who shares, "I have never experienced the cherished, valued affection from a man." There are many never-marrieds who have yet to look deeply into a relationship with another human being and see themselves mirrored back in knowingness. Or Shannon, who like thirty-eight percent of devastatingly lonely moms today[8] longs for a mom-friend to walk with her through the unending challenges of raising kids. Or Jill who admits, "I feel so lonely when I haven't heard from anyone for days."

Relational Loneliness in Scripture

Relational loneliness is so painful because, bottom line, we weren't meant to live alone. God made us to be in relationship. The need is built into our core DNA as described in Genesis 2:18, "The LORD God said, 'It is not good for the man to be alone. I will make a helper suitable for him.'" The word *helper* actually means "strong warrior," and is used of God for Israel. God made Eve for Adam, bone of his bone and flesh of his flesh (Genesis 2:23). She was perfect for him, and he was perfect for her.

Were they soul mates? Each other's "person"? Genesis 2:24 describes Adam and Eve as "one flesh," before the fall of mankind. But afterward? It's doubtful. Scripture is clear that there would be strife in their relationship (Genesis 3:16).

From the first marriage onward, the Old Testament shares the woes of mismatched relationships. In a patriarchal society where a man's lineage and a woman's worth were provided through children, the lack of love in marriage was less important than the lack of heirs. Understandably then, the struggle to procreate broke as many relationships as it created.

- Abraham and Sarah waited for decades to become parents, with Sarah taking matters into her own hands using her handmaiden, Hagar, to get the job done (Genesis 16).
- As the beloved of Jacob, second-wife Rachel

longed for children while the cast-aside first wife was abundantly fruitful (Genesis 29–30).
- In contrast to her husband's other childbearing wife, the infertile Hannah wept for children before God in 1 Samuel 1–3.

To such a backdrop, the Psalmist writes what some believe to be a poem of Israel returning from exile to Babylon. The oppressed are restored. The solitary ones—widows and orphans and those without children—are put in homes with others to live. "A father to the fatherless, a defender of widows, is God in his holy dwelling. God sets the lonely in families" (Psalm 68:5–6).

A similar restoration is portrayed in Psalm 113:9 where, "[God] settles the childless woman in her home as a happy mother of children."

Yet to many, these words are promises of what is yet to come, not what is currently experienced.

In the New Testament, Jesus enters a world that devalues whole elements of humankind. In the first century, women and children were seen as possessions, deriving value only when producing heirs or when coming of age or when born as male. Within the parameters of Jewish law, the diseased and disabled held no value and were seen as unclean and rejected from the community.

In contrast to the diminishment of so many, Jesus embraces humankind, claiming every individual as His creation, His beloved, His very own. Consider:

- He spoke in public to a Samaritan woman who had been in many relationships—while others avoided or rejected her (John 4:1–26).
- He raised the dead son of a widow back to life

when otherwise the mother would have been without family and without provision (Luke 7:11–17).

- While dying on the cross, He assigned His disciple John to adopt His own mother into his family (John 19:26–27).

Jesus loved people. He loved individuals. Families. Marriages. Friends. Disciples. Men. Women. Children. He healed the demon-possessed that they might be restored to their right mind (Luke 8:2, Luke 9:37–43) and able to enjoy healthy relationships. He restored a woman suffering from an issue of blood, which had made her untouchable, so she could return to relationships with others (Matthew 9:20–22). When a paralyzed man called for help because he had no one to help him get into the healing waters of a pool, Jesus became the friend who carried him to healing, healing him himself (John 5:7). And when Jesus spoke final words to His closest disciples in the upper room before going to the cross, He promised them, "I will not leave you as orphans; I will come to you" (John 14:18).

Though at times He was lonely himself on this planet, Jesus enjoyed a constant relationship with His Father. "A time is coming . . . when you will be scattered, each to your own home. You will leave me all alone. Yet I am not alone, for my Father is with me" (John 16:32). This is God's created intent for us all. "My prayer is not for them alone. I pray also for those who will believe in me through their message, that all of them may be one, Father, just as you are in me and I am in you" (John 17:20–21).

Jesus modeled a relational belonging that resulted from being known by His Father. How can we experience such security?

Relationships and Our Faith

The arc of the Bible reveals that we can experience the pain of alone without relationships, and often, even with them. It's true that God points to His provision of the church as His solution for our relational need. Paul describes the interdependence of each of us in the church in 1 Corinthians 12:14–27.

> Even so the body is not made up of one part but of many.
>
> Now if the foot should say, "Because I am not a hand, I do not belong to the body," it would not for that reason stop being part of the body. And if the ear should say, "Because I am not an eye, I do not belong to the body," it would not for that reason stop being part of the body. If the whole body were an eye, where would the sense of hearing be? If the whole body were an ear, where would the sense of smell be? But in fact God has placed the parts in the body, every one of them, just as he wanted them to be. If they were all one part, where would the body be? As it is, there are many parts, but one body.
>
> The eye cannot say to the hand, "I don't need you!" And the head cannot say to the feet, "I don't need you!" On the contrary, those parts of the body that seem to be weaker are indispensable, and the parts that we think are less honorable we treat with special honor. And the parts that are unpresentable are treated with special modesty, while our presentable parts need no special treatment. But God has put the body together, giving greater honor to the parts that lacked it, so that there should be no division in the body, but that its parts should have equal concern for each other. If one

part suffers, every part suffers with it; if one part is
honored, every part rejoices with it.

Now you are the body of Christ, and each one of
you is a part of it.

On and on, throughout the New Testament epistles, from
Paul to Peter and James, you'll note a strong emphasis on the
importance of remaining in healthy and truthful relationships
with one another in the church, THE place we can go to meet
our relational needs as brothers and sisters in Christ.

But here's the thing. People, even followers of Christ, are
imperfect. Just as Adam and Eve fell and broke away from
relationship with God, so have we. And because we have
broken from God, we will experience brokenness with each
other. Even in the church.

God's answer to our relational loneliness is not so much
about finding our "person" or even our "people." Rather,
God woos us to understand that our core need for connection to people begins with our connection to Him, the One
who knows us—who perfectly *perceives* us.

I Know You Because I Made You

God is the One who knows us. Each of us. Through and
through.

At first, we can pull back from the intimacy of God
"knowing us." He knows us? We might panic, pulling up
the covers and diving deep to avoid His gaze. Surely, if God
knows us, then He couldn't possibly love what He knows?

Psalm 139 describes David's secure grasp of God's uncon-
ditionally loving knowledge of him. Note that David writes
from a context where he's struggling with evil enemies who,
if they searched him, would use every discovery for his

downfall. David comforts himself with the contrast of a God who searches David's life with only a goal of good—and in a relationship of unconditional love.

Beginning and ending this Psalm of confidence is David's invitation to God to "search me." To *search* here means to "closely examine me, study me."

What does David discover as he invites God's search?

First, in verses one through six David discovers that God knows him. God really, truly knows David.

> You have searched me, LORD,
> and you *know* me.
> You know when I sit and when I rise;
> you *perceive* my thoughts from afar.
> You *discern* my going out and my lying down;
> you are *familiar* with all my ways.
> Before a word is on my tongue
> you, LORD, *know* it completely.
> You hem me in behind and before,
> and you lay your hand upon me.
> Such knowledge is too wonderful for me,
> too lofty for me to attain.

Look back over each word that I've emphasized with italics in the verses above.

Know: Here is God's full, personal awareness of David, based on a thorough search of his heart and mind.

Perceive: God carefully considers David's every-minute thoughts.

Discern: The root of this word means "to scatter or sift, to fan apart, to winnow." God sifts through David's every action and understands all David is and all that he does— even before David is aware.

Familiar: God is intimately acquainted with everything about David.

One commentator summarizes, "David professes that the Lord has complete knowledge of him—his movements, his thoughts, and his words."[9]

David knows that God knows him completely: David, the tender shepherd. David, the musician. David, the tortured-by-Saul. David, the king. David, the adulterer with Bathsheba. David, the murderer of Uriah. David, the beloved by God.

What freedom! Knowing that God intimately knows us can change the way we live. We can dare to invite Him to "search" us and confidently grant Him entrance into every part of our being. Once there, we can give ourselves over to the privilege of being known by our loving God.

In verses thirteen through seventeen, David next discovers that God knows—perceives—him because God made him.

> For you *created* my inmost being;
> you *knit* me together in my mother's womb.
> I praise you because I am fearfully
> and wonderfully made;
> your works are wonderful,
> I know that full well.
> My frame was not hidden from you
> when I was made in the secret place,
> when I was *woven* together in the depths of the earth.
> Your eyes saw my unformed body;
> all the days ordained for me were written in your book
> before one of them came to be.
> How precious to me are your thoughts, God!
> How vast is the sum of them!

Note the italicized words again. The concept of Psalm 139:13–15 is that of being knit, woven, embroidered together as in how David's very skeleton and being were formed. In a secret place of creation, God stitched David into existence. As He does with each of us. He knows us because He made us.

My grandmother was a talented seamstress who as a teen won contests in her native Texas. Throughout my life, she celebrated hallmark occasions with a hand-sewn gift. A burgundy mohair sweater for my high school graduation. A turquoise quilt for my marriage. I'd fold over a corner of each custom-crafted item to discover her signature tag reading, "Handmade for you by Munna."

Imagine a tag embroidered at the back of your neck, permanently pronouncing how God sees you: "Handmade with love by God." Wow! That's how God viewed David. And that's how God views each of us.

A slight tweak on the beloved song, "Jesus Loves Me This I Know" rearranges the words with a startling revelation: *Jesus knows me, this I love.* Yes! Our God knows us—perceives us—because God made us. Therefore, He is uniquely positioned to be our ultimate "Person."

Ahhhh. It's from a foundation of being known and loved that we can venture into relationship with other people, those God can use to ease our relational loneliness. And safely held in God's knowledge of us, we might also risk being used of God to soothe the relational loneliness of others as we offer ourselves as one of their "persons." "Relationships don't come in packages of perfection," Lysa TerKeurst reminds us. "Relationships come in packages of potential."[10]

Above my desk today is a framed cardboard card—cut

from the top of a gift box—covered with the handwriting of both my mother and my father. The story behind it is that they hadn't yet selected a name for their second-born daughter when I arrived. In the hospital room, my dad grabbed a gift box, tore off its lid and with my mom, they began the work of conjugating a name for me. Ilesa. Ilisha. Melissa. Milesa. Mellisa. Ilisa.

And yes, Alissa.

Then, in the upper right corner, sitting alone but repeated several lines down, Elisa. My parents, married only nine years in total and divorced when I was five, invested intentionality in naming me. The name they picked meant something to them. It meant something to me. So, it mattered to me that Miss Hailey mispronounced my name. Her error made me feel like an error.

I've come to realize that not only does God know my name and how to pronounce it but He also knows who I am behind its label. Jesus speaks of himself as the Good Shepherd who lays down his life for His sheep. "He calls his own sheep by name and leads them out" (John 10:3).

Once I discovered God's great and unchanging love for me, I was able to remember back to Miss Hailey and see her mistake with grace. Miss Hailey didn't mean to demean me or cause damage to my heart. I know that now. Likely, her insistence on her mispronunciation of "Alissa" grew out of self-defense, a desire to protect a space of wounding in her own being.

At the end of my fifth-grade year, Miss Hailey became engaged to be married. A few months later, from my lofty sixth-grade stature, I learned that once married, her name became Mrs. Gross. I confess, I giggled over that.

Do you know Who knows your name, its proper pronunciation, and who you are behind the label? No matter who has missed knowing us in our past or who "misses" our need to be known in our present, we can live life "unlonely" when we live in a relationship of being known and loved by our good God. He knows us—our name and the rest of us.

PRACTICE
Personalize Psalm 139

Read through Psalm 139 and insert your own name, or the personal pronouns "me" and "my," "mine" and "I." Listen to how the meaning deepens! Try this with other Scriptures as well.

You have searched _____, LORD,
and you know _____.
You know when _____ sit(s) and when _____ rise(s);
you perceive _____ thoughts from afar.
You discern _____ going out and _____ lying down;
you are familiar with all _____ ways.
Before a word is on _____ tongue
you, LORD, know it completely.
You hem _____ in behind and before,
and you lay your hand upon _____.
Such knowledge is too wonderful for _____,
too lofty for _____ to attain.

Where can _____ go from your Spirit?
Where can _____ flee from your presence?
If _____ go up to the heavens, you are there;
If _____ make my bed in the depths, you are there.
If _____ rise on the wings of the dawn,
if _____ settle on the far side of the sea,

even there your hand will guide _____,
your right hand will hold _____ fast.
If I say, "Surely the darkness will hide _____
and the light become night around _____,"
even the darkness will not be dark to you;
the night will shine like the day,
for darkness is as light to you.

For you created _____ inmost being;
you knit _____ together in _____ mother's womb.
I praise you because_____ am fearfully
and wonderfully made;
your works are wonderful,
_____ know that full well.
_____ frame was not hidden from you
when _____ was made in the secret place,
when _____ was woven together in the
depths of the earth.
Your eyes saw _____ unformed body;
all the days ordained for_____ were written
in your book
before one of them came to be.
How precious to _____ are your thoughts, God!
How vast is the sum of them!

What feelings arise as you personalize these words? Can you identify new discoveries about how God perceives you? Consider what it means that God knows you this intimately? That He calls you by name so personally?

4

God's Purpose

*"The past six months I have been prayerful (and
honestly, tearful) about my longing to lead. Such a
lonely season in my life, and I know God knows."*
—Cheryl

Our Struggle: My life has no meaning.
God's Affirmation: I know the plans I have for you.

As I pushed my cart down the grocery store aisle, peer-
ing bleakly at the jars of sauces and pastas, I noticed a
gnawing discontent hollowing into my heart. I'd run out to
pick up something to make for dinner, leaving the kids with
their dad, and it was nice to have the moment on my own.
Yet, what was this emotion that seemed to weigh down my
soul with despair? I dug about for some handhold on the
thought just below the surface of my consciousness and
pulled it out. *Why do I have to be the one to feed everyone? I
feel so depleted, with nothing left to give. Could someone feed
me? Oh, how this mother needs a break!*

I felt so alone. Lonely in my mothering and in my life.
What? I'd waited for *years* to become a mom! Oh, the

ache to be a parent while all around me, every woman I knew seemed to burst into the bloom of pregnancy. Attending baby showers, enduring Mother's Day after Mother's Day, never being a mom myself, I felt alone—set apart, different from everyone else. I loved my job teaching at a local college and counseling students. But my heart struggled in the loneliness of infertility and cried in pain for a baby.

What was wrong with me? I'd finally received my longed-for children through adoption and left my job to focus on them. I felt truly satisfied with our now-family-of-four: my dear husband, daughter, and son. The toddler/preschool years were busy, and I was tired, but I enjoyed the bustle and being needed.

So, why this malaise in the middle of the grocery store aisle?

It took me years—and rounds of counseling—to process that moment. Actually, both of those lonely moments: the longing before having children and the longing after becoming a mom. Before I was a mother, I longed for the meaning motherhood would provide, yet I found purpose in my work. After I was a mother, I loved its meaning, yet I longed for the more familiar significance of work.

Eventually I discovered that at the core of my being is a powerful desire to *matter*. To make a difference. To have purpose in my life. When I don't sense such meaning, I feel out of sorts. Set apart. Alone. Lonely.

I'm not the only one lonely in this way.

Vocational Loneliness

Every person longs for meaning. We were made to matter. From the moment God created humans and assigned them the responsibility to bear children and to care for the planet

3

God's Perception

"I feel lonely when there is no one to talk to,
when I believe no one understands me."
—Tracie

Our Struggle: No one knows the real me.
God's Affirmation: I know you because I made you.

Just before I started fifth grade, our single-mom family moved from the San Francisco Bay Area to suburban Houston. I was already reeling as a ten-year-old experiencing pubescent mood swings and a spike of growth taking me to 5' 2"—way above most girls my age. While at the time I had no idea that I'd only grow one more inch over my whole lifetime, in that season I felt giant-like around other kids. Moving across the country added an extra dose of anxiety as I would need to make all new friends in a strange place.

So, when I entered Miss Hailey's fifth-grade classroom, clad in my supercool white go-go boots and puff-sleeved mini dress, I was more than a little bit nervous. Did girls wear such trends in Texas? Would I fit in or stand out?

I tucked my long legs under my desk and sat obediently

and its inhabitants (Genesis 1:28–30), men and women were christened with the call toward purpose. Sure, our choice to separate ourselves from God by choosing our way rather than His way has resulted in confusion and distortion of our meaning. But we are still made for a purpose that provides us with meaning.

This purpose is called *vocation*. The word comes from the Latin *vox*, and means "voice, a call, a summons." Often the concept of vocation is applied to occupation or work, as in "a strong feeling of suitability for a particular career." In the Christian worldview, vocation can apply to our mission, calling, function, or purpose.[1]

How does vocational loneliness develop in our days?

In his book *The Courage to Be*, theologian Paul Tillich argued that the thing people of all ages are most afraid of is *emptiness*. We struggle to shake the feeling that our days are purposeless, and we are beset by the "anxiety about the loss of an ultimate concern, a meaning which gives meaning to all meanings."[2]

Various issues bring about vocational loneliness.

Uncertainty about our contributions. What are our strengths? How does our personality best fit in a workplace or family? How do we turn everyday skills into market-able assets—duties we can be paid for? Eva would love to turn her hobby of wreath-making, gift-wrapping, and accessory-making into a paying pastime. But the unending care of her kids and the lack of start-up funds and tech know-how hold her back in uncertainty.

Closed doors to our investment. Whether due to our gender, our background, our race, our values, our age, or other characteristics, we may experience an exclusion from the vocation to which we feel called. Suzanne loves to teach the Bible and offers small group studies to the women in her neighborhood. She longs to be included in the weekly study classes at her church but can't seem to gain the attention of the pastoral staff. She guesses it's because of her lack of formal training . . . and perhaps her gender.

Stunted vocational development. We may long to grow in a certain capacity but lack the funds for education or the courage to seek out a mentor or the network to connect with opportunities. Marilyn has repeatedly applied for various promotions, only to be overlooked because she is uncredentialed in her field. More schooling would require her to step back from her current responsibilities—an impossibility if she's to meet her bills.

Comparison that results in self-disqualification. We look around at others, whether on social media or in real life, and conclude that our offerings are too meager, or they are not pretty, smart, trendy, or valuable enough to matter. As a result, we pull back our potential contributions. My heart hurts as I recall conversation after conversation with gifted women who long to bring forth their gifts but feel that what they have to contribute isn't significant enough to warrant inclusion.

At some point—often at many points—in our lives, we all experience this type of loneliness.

When have you experienced vocational loneliness? Perhaps you've struggled to find your purpose in relationships—as a daughter or sister or wife or mother or stepmom. It may be that you stare at closed doors in your profession, uninvited into places of influence you long to occupy. Maybe you've been overburdened by responsibilities that don't seem to "fit" who you really are yet you possess zero bandwidth to pursue a different path. Or it could be that you've moved beyond the years of vital contribution into a smaller world where your offering is now undefined, unseen, or unnoticed.

For me in the grocery store aisle, amidst jars of sauce and boxes of pasta, my filled-to-full mothering heart overflowed into my emptier-than-empty more-than-a-mom being. I had quit my job in order to mother. But in that moment, my mothering satisfaction simply didn't complete the need of my career calling. Before I was a mom, my career calling didn't fill up my mothering vacuum. In both situations I was vocationally lonely. I had yet to discover how to address the multi-layered need for vocation in my being.

Vocational Loneliness in the Bible

Core to our experience of vocational loneliness is the reality that we were made for meaning, yet that created call has been disrupted by the fall. Genesis tells the story of our vocational call and also describes the entrance of vocational loneliness. As noted above, God created us to bear children and to care for our planet and its inhabitants (Genesis 1:28). When we turned from God's ways to our own, vocational strife entered with the result of great struggle and strife in our purpose-filled work (Genesis 3:14–19). Ever since, we have wrestled with our vocational offering, often experiencing instead the vocational loneliness of unfulfilled life purpose.

Consider some residents in Scripture who suffered vocational loneliness. For forty years, Moses tended his father-in-law's sheep in what Chuck Swindoll called "the backside of the desert," far removed from the lavish lifestyle and leadership influence he enjoyed when he was raised as an adopted son in Pharaoh's palace. Witnessing the suffering of the Israelites and then losing his temper and murdering an Egyptian meant Moses would hide out for decades, his strong skills dormant. In Exodus 2:22, he described himself as "a foreigner in a foreign land," and that he was. Until in Exodus 3, where we find Moses beckoned by God to a burning bush, receiving a new call to lead Israel out of slavery.

David was anointed king of Israel at the age of sixteen but then not crowned for nearly fourteen years as he coped with King Saul's jealousy and instability. During much of this season, Saul "kept David with him and would not let him return home to his family" (1 Samuel 18:2). And at Saul's direction, David succeeded in every military effort, and Saul rewarded him with a high rank in the army (1 Samuel 18:5). But Saul also tried to kill David both in the palace and in his own house (1 Samuel 19:10–11). Thus, while anointed as king, many of David's more powerful gifts remained unused until eventually Saul died and David assumed the throne.

Times of preparation also contributed to vocational loneliness when individuals lived in a "now but not yet" season. Paul spent three years somewhere in Arabia before arriving in Jerusalem, and then he spent a few weeks with Peter and James, the brother of Jesus, (Galatians 1:17–20). Fourteen more years passed before he presented himself as a follower of Christ to the other disciples in Jerusalem (Galatians 2:1). When he did arrive, he writes in 2:2, "I went in response to a revelation and, meeting privately with those esteemed as leaders, I presented to them the gospel that I preach among the Gentiles. I wanted to be sure I was not running and had not been running my race in vain." Note that Paul, who would become a central leader of the church, humbled himself and his leadership gifts to the leadership of others.

We see a kind of vocational loneliness even in our Lord as He struggled alone in the garden—ignored by His closest disciples and writhing in pain at the anticipation of the Father's abandonment on the cross (Luke 22:39–44).

Lysa TerKeurst helps us understand the confusion of vocational loneliness: "To be set aside is to be rejected. To be set apart is to be given an assignment that requires preparation.[3]

The long wait for vocational preparation and placement can result in vocational loneliness.

Vocation and Our Faith

Something stirs inside me when I consider the word *vocation*. Something lofty. Something appealing. I reach for it.

I discover that there is a general, or universal, element to vocation. We are all first called *to* God, to be image-bearers and to live in relationship to the One who created us. This core calling is vital for our understanding of vocation. It's the calling of Genesis 1–3 where we are made in God's image and to be in relationship with Him.

Os Guinness put it this way in his book *The Call*, "Calling is the truth that God calls us to himself so decisively that everything we are, everything we do, and everything we have is invested with a special devotion, dynamism, and direction lived out as a response to his summons and service."[4] Dietrich Bonhoeffer expressed a similar understanding, "The calling is the call of Jesus Christ to belong wholly to him; it is the laying claim to me by Christ at the place at which this call has found me."[5]

In addition to the general or universal vocational call, there is also a particular or specific vocational calling on our lives, something—often many things—we are uniquely created to accomplish as we live out our relationship with God. In this way, we are called *for* our God—to live out who we are in what we do for Him in our world.

The Denver Institute for Faith and Work exists to help

Christians discover their calling and to live it out through their work. Regarding this specific or personal vocation, they suggest, "God is forming each of us to live an *unrepeatable* life—each of us has gifts and aptitudes and experiences to contribute something, however small, in service of God and neighbor that cannot be duplicated by anybody else. Personal stewardship means taking responsibility for the work which cannot be done by anyone else."[6] Pretty powerful!

Just as we saw vocational loneliness lived out in many individuals in Scripture, so we see both these levels of vocational call in various biblical characters. Jesus first called His disciples *to* himself in John 1, "Come" (v. 39), "Follow me" (v. 43), "Come, follow me" (Matthew 4:19). On the road to Damascus, He appeared to Saul, transforming him to Paul (Acts 9:1–19). And to you and me, He says "Come to me . . ." (Matthew 11:28).

Also, God calls His followers *for* specific purposes. Moses, David, and Paul as already described. But also, Abraham was called to become a great nation (Genesis 12:1–3), Joshua to take Israel into the promised land (Joshua 1:1–6), Rahab to protect the spies (Joshua 2:1–24), Mary to be the mother of Jesus (Luke 1:26–38), Peter to be a leader in the church, (Matthew 16:18), and on and on and on.

The first-century disciples, and you and I as twenty-first century followers, are called generally first *to* Jesus, "Come to me . . ." (Matthew 11:28), to become His children (1 John 3:1). We are further called specifically *for* Him, to "go and make disciples of all nations, baptizing them in the name of the Father and the Son and of the Holy Spirit, and teaching them to obey everything I have commanded you" (Matthew 28:19–20).

So how do we move from the loneliness of vocational

uncertainty to vocational fulfillment? We first receive and respond to the general call *to* be in relationship with God through Jesus. Our core offering always grows from this core commitment. And then, once secured in this relationship, we ask God to show us His other, specific calling *for* Him in our world.

I Know the Plans I Have for You

When I graduated from college, I struggled with what would be "next" for me. Having ended a long-term romantic relationship, I felt the loneliness and uncertainty of my newly unattached status. I rested securely in my relationship with God (my general call to God). I loved Him and lived for Him. But I wrestled with the "more" of my life's meaning. What would become of me? What would I do with the rest of my life? Was there something specific I was called to do? At twenty-two, I had barely started out in life, and the years—decades—yawned before me like a new journal. Blank page after blank page. Why was I here? What was my purpose?

While I didn't recognize it at the time, I was seeking my specific vocation. Where had He called me to go *for* Him?

One day, a wise mentor showed up at my dorm room door with the gift of a colorful plaque containing calligraphy words, "'For I know the plans I have for you,' declares the LORD, 'plans to prosper you and not to harm you, plans to give you hope and a future'" (Jeremiah 29:11).

Before that time, I'd never noticed this verse. But it sounded promising. When I moved home, I hung it over my desk and stared at it for long moments from my tilted-back chair. I'd swivel my head from the plaque before me to catch the reflection of myself in a mirror hanging to my right, considering each phrase. Plans for me. Plans to prosper me, not harm me. Plans to give me hope. Plans for a future.

For the longest time, I took that verse to heart as not just promising but as a literal promise. God had the specific plans for me, I read. The job? The place? The man? The plans?

I joined a Bible study, took a temp job working for a friend's dad, and volunteered with high schoolers. I went to church and connected with friends afterwards. I prayed God would show me the plans.

Over coffee with a friend who was headed into ministry, he asked, "When have you felt most alive in your life?" The question pried open my thoughts, and I realized I'd felt most alive when I was doing an independent study on death and dying my freshman year in college. Ironic, right? That I would feel most alive while sitting next to someone thick in the work of dying? But sitting vigil with a beautiful Black man, Mr. Hairston, as he moved from here to the hereafter, touched my soul in a powerful way. Death felt sacred. And the process of passage seemed holy. I wanted to be closer to those who suffered, to comfort, to offer presence and hope.

Plans for purpose. For meaning. For mattering. Called to God . . . and then called for God.

So, thinking I might become a hospital chaplain, I enrolled in seminary and began to consider all the angles of God's plans for me. The plans to prosper me, not harm me. Plans to give me hope. Plans for a future. I set my foot on the next place of purpose and invested there. Even though I didn't actually become a hospital chaplain, God used seminary to shape me; and after graduation, I set my foot in the next. Then in the next. Then in the next. One next after another until today I stand on layers of "nexts," all expressions of my general vocational calling, lived out in my specific vocational callings.

Since that era, I've come to understand that these words from the book of Jeremiah were spoken over an exiled Israel, offering hope and assurance that one day God's people would be rescued from domination from a foreign country and returned to their homeland, and to the heart of God. Yes, God did have a plan. It was the plan that would unfold over centuries and millennia, weaving prophecies into realities and culminating in the arrival of a Messiah who would provide the ultimate rescue and return of people to their Savior. Today, God's planned rescue continues, crossing continents and seas, connecting generation after generation of humankind to the hope and future of a relationship beyond brokenness with our loving God through Jesus.

What do these words of Jeremiah 29:11 say to us today as we struggle with the meaning of our lives? Do they relate to us a secondary application to the main meaning from the prophet to his people? I think they do. As these words fit into the overall arc of Scripture, God's encouragement to Israel can also encourage you and me. Just as He planned good for Israel, He plans good for us. He knows all plans for all of us. He uses all things for our good (Romans 8:28). Because He is God over all, and He is good.

Now, decades past that awkward aloneness of my early twenties, I can look back and see God's plans lived out in my life.

Who knew that some forty-five years ago in a high school English class, as I pulled out a spiral notebook and poised my Bic ballpoint over the even blue lines to catalog various ponderings on paper, those would be my writing beginnings?

Who knew that as I raised my hand as a sixteen-year-old to

my church's invitation to join their youth leadership, ordaining me as an elder at that tender age, leadership was in store for me later?

Who knew I would turn the direction of my life toward full-time ministry when as a green graduate from the University of Texas, I searched the horizons for a place to grow my "next" and settled on Denver Seminary?

Who knew I'd meet the man I'd later marry on a fall morning in Old Testament class?

Who knew I'd sit in the foothills office of a local college president and agree to serve as that school's dean of women?

Who knew I'd dare to write a book about the challenges of waiting for *everything* to come to be?

Who knew I'd receive first one tiny baby girl and then her to-be baby brother through adoption?

All these were layers of being called *to* God and then called *for* Him.

Another one came . . .

Who knew I'd answer the phone one spring day to hear an invitation to apply to become the first president of MOPS—Mothers of Preschoolers International?

That one really threw me. When I received a phone call from a board member of that international grassroots movement of moms, I cowered at the thought. Me? From the broken family? Me? Who'd never even been pregnant? Me? Lead a mothering organization?

Besides doubling up my therapy sessions, I hunkered down in Scripture—right where I'd been reading—and took in the day's passage from John 15 where Jesus spoke to His disciples in the upper room. Preparing them for ministry in the days after His departure, He said, "I chose you and appointed you so that you might go and bear fruit—fruit that will last" (John 15:16).

God knew. *I know the plans I have for you . . . plans to prosper you and not to harm you, plans to give you a future and a hope.* As He did for Israel. As He did for me.

Those called *to* Him are also called *for* Him.

There have been many detours along the way. Disappointments. Let downs. Giant potholes of trials. Surprising turns. And delightful unveilings of what I'd never expected.

After my twenty-year tenure leading MOPS, I struggled to find a next "next" to place my foot. I remember sensing the nudge to say yes to *everything* that first year—opening doors all around me in hopes that one would bring a "fit."

What an adventure!

I spoke on national stages before tens of thousands. I traveled to Africa with American mom-bloggers, and together we wrote about our experiences with the ONE Campaign to address poverty and disease in sub-Saharan Africa to over a million moms back home. I brought home first one and then a second Rottweiler. I continued grand-mothering my first grandson and became a grandmother a second time. I watched my son marry.

In those years, a strange yearning would not be silenced. It was an antsy, itchy distraction that propelled me at times into an unnecessary busyness. An untethered floating in the atmosphere as if I were cut off from my mothership. A friend observed, "Elisa, you seem to be desperate to attach to something. What is it that you're reaching for?" And I realized the answer to her kind-yet-corrective question. I was reaching for some*thing* rather than some*One*.

It was as if I'd focused only on the call *for* God and had forgotten I was first called *to* His heart.

"Attach yourself to Me," God wooed me forward.

Who knew? God knew.

When I lose my way . . .

when I worry about my world . . .
when I question my offering . . .
when I fret about the future . . .
when I struggle to continue . . .
when I suffer in loneliness . . .
when I wrestle with doubts . . .
when I decide I'm done . . .

may I remember that God knew, and may I trust that He still knows.

God knows me—and He knows the plans He has for me. And for you as well.

PRACTICE
Create Your Own "Who Knew?" List

Begin with as early as you can remember and bring forward the vocational moments of your life. What roles did you occupy in elementary, middle, and high school? How did you lead or follow in your family of origin? What relational places have you occupied as an adult? What jobs have you held?

Now enlarge your list into your own "Who Knew the Plans He Had for Me?" list

Who knew _____?
Who knew _____?
Who knew _____?
God knew!

5

God's Presence

"I sometimes wonder if God is listening."
—Lyn

Our Struggle: I feel so alone.
God's Affirmation: I will be with you.

As I've shared, I went through lonely seasons as a child. Not lonely in the classic way where I wandered my neighborhood trying to draw the attention of someone who might chat with me. And not bored where I simply fell into long hours of doldrumy nothingness. It's more that I was often left alone, and while that wasn't horrible all the time as I imagined friends and games to entertain myself, there was an unhingedness to my soul. A not-belongingness. A lack of connection to concrete care. My mother's disease distracted her. My father was absent. My sister and brother fought their own battles for identity and belonging. Teachers were teachers. Friends helped . . . but it depended on who and what they were up to. Sometimes I could forge my way "in" to friendships, but other times I felt excluded.

I wanted something more. More meaning. More certainty.

More security. The "more" I longed for honestly didn't seem to have much to do with people.

In my teen years, I came to understand there was "more" in my relationship with God than just loving Him as my heavenly Father, and I embraced His love for me in providing Jesus as my Savior. Then, one night shortly after this enlightenment, I had a dream. It was an out-of-body experience where I saw myself falling off a high cliff into what looked to be flesh-colored rocks far below. But as I landed, the rocks surprised me with their cushiony softness. They were not rocks after all, but rather the huge hands of God. I heard a voice saying, "I am your heavenly Father—I will never leave you nor forsake you."

I awoke, and wondered at the meaning. As I look back on that moment, I think it was the first time I began to consider the ongoing presence of God in my life. That He was truly more than just something I could turn to when needed. He was a personal God I could do life with. All of it. All the time. 24-7. A constant presence for me.

I had loved God as Father. I had embraced Jesus as His Son and my Savior. It was hard for me to put words to it in that season, but looking back, I can see that I was beginning to encounter the Holy Spirit. With His help, I would come to experience a spiritual belonging I'd never before known I needed.

Ahhh. Maybe this was the "more" I so longed for?

Spiritual Loneliness

Have you ever felt lonely spiritually? The dawning realization that it's basically just *you* in life. You in the morning. You in the day. You in the evening. You when you turn out the lights and slip into sleep. And then you awake. Just you again. You feel *so alone.*

Spiritual loneliness is an experience of ultimate emptiness and incompleteness. It's not about being loved, being known in a meaningful relationship or having a life purpose. Rather, this type of loneliness is the sense of being alone on the grand scale of things—the untethered experience of living without a connection to our ultimate Source who created us: God.

Spiritual loneliness can result from at least six realities.

Life without God. Most obvious is the reality that before we know God, we can't know our true relationship and connection to Him. And before we turn to Him to redeem us, we remain spiritually alone. The prophet Isaiah expresses our experience of being cut off from God due to our choices against Him and His ways. "Your iniquities have separated you from God; your sins have hidden his face from you, so that he will not hear" (Isaiah 59:2). Void of His promise, perception, and purpose, we float. Our life is a vapor.

As I've already described, before I knew God as Father, as Savior, and as Spirit, I experienced an utterly lost longing for "more."

Looking for "more" in all the wrong places. Even after we come to know God, we can forget to look to Him to fill our deepest needs and instead look to more temporary fixes. We might not notice at first as we become so accustomed to assuaging our spiritual longing with media, food, work, and even healthy relationships like marriage or children or grandchildren. But when one of these elements prioritizes over the lasting filling only God can provide, our hearts may cave into emptiness again.

Lysa TerKeurst writes, "How dangerous it is when our

souls are gasping for God but we're too distracted flirting with the world to notice."[1]

Being the "only one." Living as an "only believer" in a world that doesn't recognize God can leave us spiritually lonely. Lyn writes, "My loneliness comes from being the only one in my family that cries out to [God] . . . I desperately want someone at home to pray with me. My heart aches because I carry this burden alone."

I remember when I tried to explain my faith to my father on one of his rare "dinner visits" —when my older sister and I went to dinner with our dad and stepmother. We sawed at our steaks and tried to hold up our end of adult-like conversation. His response to my awe-filled testimony about Jesus? "You don't have to become a nun, you know." Huh?

This "only one" kind of spiritual loneliness catches our hearts when we work in an environment that excludes faith, when our friends leave God out of their lives, and when we live in a world where it's more common to trust in trends, science, or government than God.

Loss. Life's tragedies can unmoor us and set us adrift spiritually. Kathy shares that after her fifty-three-year marriage ended in her husband's sudden death, she gradually began to redefine her connection to God only to find herself isolated once again, this time in the wake of the COVID-19 pandemic. "It was instantly over. Pulled out from under me like a rug!"

When my daughter delivered our grandson, Malachi, he passed straight from her womb into heaven. God helped me rally in the moment, offering prayers for my daughter, son-in-law, and other grandson as they reeled in their new reality. I was able to steward his little body for a short hour as his mother was being attended to with her husband. And the following day, I managed to show up with bits and pieces of hope for what God might provide next. But in the next weeks, the anguish of his too-short appearance on this planet left me mired in bed, unable to reach to God for more than just the next breath. I knew He was there, but I couldn't seem to experience His presence.

The grief of death, divorce, the loss of a child, even unemployment can leave us unanchored and alone. We wonder how God could allow such suffering. Where has God gone?

Illness. Physical disease, disability, and diminishment can cut us off from experiencing God's presence. Stricken with cancer, we endure chemo or radiation alone. Recovering from surgery or an accident, we wake to discover each day that the task of healing before us is something no one can share with us. If we do not sense God near us in our plight, our aloneness carves out a deep spiritual longing.

When my husband contracted a life-threatening blood infection, I was thousands of miles away in another country serving a ministry. Alone, he was forced to manage his own care from his ICU bed. While I could FaceTime and interact with his doctors, the burden of both recovery and care-management fell to Evan. He felt so alone in the wee hours when no one else was awake. When he couldn't reach his phone. When he couldn't stop the fevered shaking. Even though he knew I was on my way to him and that God was all around him, he felt alone.

I've not often been ill, but even a brief bout with the flu—the humiliating hunching over the toilet and the incapacitating revolution of chills and fevers—has taught me well the lonely work of the infirmed. "Where is God when it hurts?" author Philip Yancey asks the question of all who are so stricken.

Silence. Some refer to seasons of silence—when we long to hear from God but can't—as "the dark night of the soul."

In such hours, days and months, God seems to go underground. Unanswered prayers. Unmet needs. Wandering minds. Worrisome thoughts. Untethered emotions. Silence reverberates all around us.

In the challenges of my children's wanderings, in a family member's addiction, in a coworker's choice against my leadership, and in confusing financial turns—God's silence has screamed. In such moments, it can seem as if God is mocking our humanity, pushing us further and further away from His Being and the connection to Him we desire.

Spiritual Loneliness in Scripture

When I think of spiritual loneliness in Scripture, I go straight to Job. I mean . . . !

In the first chapter, Job discovers:

- Enemies stole the livestock of his sons and daughters and then killed their servants (1:13–15).
- Fire of God burned up other livestock and more servants (1:16).
- Raiding parties killed all the camels and more servants (1:17).
- A mighty desert wind collapsed the house on his sons and daughters, killing them all (1:18–19).

Job's response? He is faithful. "Naked I came from my mother's womb, and naked I will depart. The Lord gave and the Lord has taken away; may the name of the Lord be praised," (1:21). Over the next many chapters, Job's friends sit and listen, and his wife challenges Job to walk away from God, yet Job tenaciously clings to his belief that God is just and loving and true.

Between his statements of faithfulness, though, we can see Job struggling with what could be described as a version of spiritual loneliness.

> If only I knew where to find him; if only I could go to his dwelling! I would state my case before him and fill my mouth with arguments. . . . "But if I go to the east, he is not there; if I go to the west, I do not find him. When he is at work in the north, I do not see him; when he turns to the south, I catch no glimpse of him." (Job 23:3–9)

Still, Job remains confident in God, "But he knows the way that I take; when he has tested me, I will come forth as gold" (Job 23:10). Sure enough, God restores abundance to Job—even more than he'd experienced before (Job 42:12).

Being confident in God doesn't necessarily mean we won't experience His seeming absence, His distance, His silence, and therefore a deep spiritual loneliness.

The psalms reveal valleys of spiritual loneliness where God's voice seems silent and His presence removed. Psalm 88 has been described as "the darkest Psalm in the Psalter."[2]

> May my prayer come before you; turn your ear to my cry. I am overwhelmed with troubles and my life draws near to death. I am counted among those who go down to the pit; I am like one without strength. I am set apart with the dead, like the slain who lie in the grave, whom you remember no more, who are cut off from your care. (Psalm 88:2–5)

> But I cry to you for help, LORD; in the morning my prayer comes before you. Why, LORD, do you reject me and hide your face from me? (Psalm 88:13–14)

And didn't Jesus himself experience deep spiritual loneliness? Matthew and Mark report on His crucifixion. Here is Mark's account: "At noon, darkness came over the whole land until three in the afternoon. And at three in the afternoon Jesus cried out in a loud voice, 'Eloi, Eloi, lema sabachthani?' (which means 'My God, my God, why have you forsaken me?')" (Mark 15:33–34; see also Matthew 27:45–46). Here *forsaken* means to "desert, leave behind, forsake, abandon."[3] Truly, in this moment, Jesus experienced a deep spiritual disconnection from God—on our behalf.

Spirituality and Our Faith

Let's pause for a moment and consider: Is spiritual loneliness always a bad thing? Might running our hands along the hollow of our need reveal God and even teach us to want Him?

Perhaps spiritual loneliness, once identified, can become a pathway to God. In his book *The Eternal Now*, theologian Paul Tillich writes that the word *loneliness* is used to express the pain of being alone where *solitude* expresses the glory of being alone.[4] And just maybe, in this glory we can actually discover more and more about God. Never-married Henri Nouwen suggests, "Instead of running away from our loneliness and trying to forget it or deny it, we have to protect it and turn it into a fruitful solitude. To live a spiritual life, we must first find the courage to enter into the desert of our loneliness and to change it by gentle and persistent efforts into a garden of solitude. . . . As hard as it is to believe that the dry desolate desert can yield endless varieties of flowers, it is equally hard to imagine that our loneliness is hiding unknown beauty."[5]

As we embrace our inevitable spiritual loneliness, our aching emptiness without God, might we begin to experience the reality that we were designed for relationship with Him?

Basilea Schlink was a German Lutheran religious leader and writer who lived in community with other women, seeking God. In one season, she felt God calling her to solitude. For months she would spend her days alone in a humble room, writing and praying with God. But gradually, loneliness began to gnaw at her heart. She wrote, "The Lord in His love has planned pathways of loneliness for us, not so that our hearts will be tormented or embittered, but so that we shall seek Him and draw closer to Him."[6]

Ahhh . . . Modern-day devotional writer, Sarah Young, describes something similar, "Instead of yearning for a problem-free life, rejoice that trouble can highlight your awareness of [God's] presence."[7] When we attend to our experiences of spiritual loneliness and let them lead us to God, we may discover the "more" we long for is actually in Him and His readiness to meet our deepest needs.

I Will Be With You

My dream of falling off a cliff into the very hands of God stays with me today. I replay my slow-motion landing, oh-so-softly, into His safe hands. God's presence with me in the days/nights/weeks/months/years/decades of my life lifts me to a place of greater and greater need for just that: His presence. Living in His presence has taught me that I cannot live outside of it. Outside of Him there is no air. No ground. No being.

And yet, there are still moments when I fall in this life. I flail about, grasping for His Being beneath me and wildly clutching at the air in search of His substance. I spin and tumble upside down in the air, losing my focus, my hold, my experience of Him.

Jesus's last sentence before ascending to heaven beckons me with its offer. "And surely I am with you always, to the very end of the age" (Matthew 28:20). Here He offers a crescendo on His great commission to include us in His kingdom work when he said to, "make disciples of all nations, baptizing them . . . and teaching them to obey everything I have commanded" (28:19–20). By now the disciples are familiar with the work of the Father and the Son. And so are we. New to their understanding, and ours, is the mention of the Holy Spirit. In fact, this is one of the only times in Scripture we see mentioned the Father, Son, and Holy Spirit, all three in one breath.

Somehow, God's post-resurrection presence is uniquely experienced through the Holy Spirit. But how?

Before Jesus went to the cross, He spent a long evening in an upper room giving out directions to His disciples. John allocates four chapters to Jesus's words, which weave a message of comfort, service, preparation for persecution, exhortations about oneness, and prayers for himself, for the disciples, and for all believers to come. Central to Jesus's teaching is His presentation on the Holy Spirit: His role and work and reality in our lives.

Let's look at what Jesus says about this facet of His Being.

"I will ask the Father and he will give you another advocate to help you and be with you forever—the Spirit of truth" (John 14:16–17). Jesus does the asking of the Father, for us. Then the Father provides the Advocate to help us and be with us forever. An *advocate* is "one who takes our side and represents us as if in a legal court of law."

I will be with you. "I will not leave you as orphans; I will come to you" (John 14:18). No matter how cut off from family we may be, victims of messy marriages or children of imperfect parents, orphaned by death or orphaned by distance and dysfunction, Jesus promises to send "another" to be with us so we will not be adrift as orphans.

I will be with you. "The Advocate, the Holy Spirit, whom the Father will send in my name, will teach you all things and will remind you of everything I have said to you" (John 14:26). Back to advocacy, Jesus also reveals that the Spirit will remind us of all God has revealed of himself through Jesus. Perhaps like a built-in Google search in our hearts, the Spirit will offer ongoing access to all God has done for us and in us as a replacement for Jesus's physical presence on earth.

I will be with you. Maybe most surprising is that Jesus says, "But very truly I tell you, it is for your good that I am going away. Unless I go away, the Advocate will not come to you; but if I go, I will send him to you" (John 16:7). Jesus says it's for the *good* of the disciples, the *good* of us, that He goes away.

What? Wouldn't we rather have God with us still, in the flesh? In the passenger seat next to us—or better yet, in the driver's seat carting us about? Wouldn't we rather have God in the extra chair at our dinner tables and tucked in next to us at night? Wouldn't it be awesome if God literally appeared in the mirror right beside us each day and reminded us of His love?

Oh, but wait. That's what God did! Exactly. John writes, "The Word became flesh and made his dwelling among us" (John 1:14). At last! We are not alone but rather, God joins us *in* our world with His presence. Matthew 1:23 tells us, "'The virgin will conceive and give birth to a son, and they will call him Immanuel' (which means 'God with us')."

Yes, God came as Jesus, Immanuel, to be with humankind. To be born from a woman's womb. God scrunched himself in that small space and was born in our world in the vessel of a baby. God formed objects through the hands of a carpenter and he walked with the feet of a man. God expressed himself in the flesh, brain, and muscle of a human. Jesus's body was nailed to a cross and raised up to die in my place and in yours. Then Jesus's dead body was placed in a tomb where, after three days, God raised it from death to life while *still* containing the essence of God.

God came to be with us in Jesus to reveal himself and then provide for our great need for Him. And then, when departing to heaven, Jesus left His presence with us forever in the person of the Holy Spirit so our spiritual loneliness might, indeed, be soothed. One day, Jesus will return and be with us again. Until that time, Jesus has given us himself in the Spirit to continue to be with us.

I will be with you. Words from the Old Testament foreshadow God's coming presence. Promises made to patriarchs and prophets and psalmists.

- To Isaac, confirming His promise to Abraham: "Stay in this land for a while, and *I will be with you* and bless you" (Genesis 26:3).
- To Jacob: "Go back to the land of your fathers and to your relatives and *I will be with you*" (Genesis 31:3).
- To Moses before the Exodus: "*I will be with you*" (Exodus 3:12).
- To Joshua as he begins to lead Israel: "*I will be with you*; I will never leave you nor forsake you" (Joshua 1:5).
- To Isaiah for Israel going in to captivity: "So do not fear, for *I am with you*" (Isaiah 41:10).
- "When you pass through the waters, *I will be with you*" (Isaiah 43:2)

- "'Do not be afraid of them, for *I am with you* and will rescue you,' declares the LORD" (Jeremiah 1:8).

Into our spiritual loneliness, into our cavernous need for the very Source from which we began, God arrives with himself in the form of the Father who created and caused us, of His Son who saved us from ourselves, and of the Spirit who remains with us, present in all we do and reminding us of what we already have in our God.

So, what happens if we live like we're not alone? What if we invite the God who has promised to be with us into the everyday of our lives? I think of two ways to bring this understanding to the gaping mouth of my spiritual loneliness.

Be Present with God's Presence. Jesus's last words to His disciples were, "And surely, I am with you always, to the very end of the age" (Matthew 28:20). Might we eavesdrop in on this statement and live as if it is true for us as well? That Jesus is *with* us.

I can every day, all day, invite God's presence into my present. When I awake, I imagine Him hovering close, Jesus in the chair by the window, waiting for me to meet with Him. I get ready for the day and make room in my thoughts for Him to guide them. As I drive down the road, I put my right hand out to Him. *Guide me, I pray.* When crisis comes, when illness arrives, when tragedy strikes, I turn my first response to His presence. *Help me here!* In my conversations, my projects, my parenting, my lunch chats, my errands, my walks, I intentionally invite Him close. *Think my thoughts. Walk my steps. Be with me.* I set a place at the table for Him. I pause and thank Him for His presence at day's end as I slip into sleep.

In his book *With*, Skye Jethani suggests that instead of

life *over, under, from,* or even *for* God, what leads us into freedom and restoration is life *with* God. Yes, this is it!

Pray His Prayers. In Romans 8, Paul writes of our fundamental need in this life for help from God. His solution? Let the Spirit pray for us when we don't know what to pray.

Paul writes to those who are living in the "in between" of having assurance of life with Christ in eternity while still inhabiting this planet with all its challenges. In Romans 8:26–27, he offers clear directions for how to handle our spiritual loneliness by actually asking the Spirit for help in praying our needs.

> The Spirit helps us in our weakness. We do not know what we ought to pray for, but the Spirit himself intercedes for us through wordless groans. And he who searches our hearts knows the mind of the Spirit, because the Spirit intercedes for God's people in accordance with the will of God.

When he mentions the "Spirit helps," Paul uses a tense that is ongoing in nature. The word he's chosen here actually means to carry a heavy load. It's the same word Martha uses in John 11 when she asks Jesus to tell Mary to *help* her in her preparations.

Paul goes on to emphasize that the Spirit's help is especially available when we don't know what to pray (most of the time for many of us!). In 1 Corinthians 2:11, Paul explains how the Spirit knows what to pray when we don't. "For who knows a person's thoughts except their own spirit within them? In the same way no one knows the thoughts of God except the Spirit of God."

Isn't this amazing? When we don't know what to pray, we can ask the Spirit to pray His prayers for us. Rather than judging us as lacking, God joins us with His presence in prayer.

Can you identify moments when your spirit has longed for "more"? Like me, can you label the longing in your being where you "feel so alone" as a spiritual loneliness that only God can meet? When we see our ailment for what it is, a pathway to the "more" of God, we can steer on to its leading and in the end, discover the soothing presence of our God that He longs to provide for us by His loving Spirit.

PRACTICE
Be Present with God's Presence and Pray His Prayers

Your turn! What might happen as you walk out these concepts in your every day?

Be Present with God's Presence. Right now, put this book aside (except for these directions!) and imagine God right next to you. In the very room where you are at this moment. In the chair next to you. At the table or counter. Before the mirror. Pause to take in His presence with you. You are not alone!

Now listen carefully in your heart. What affirmation might He be offering you about His presence with you?

As you go about your day, to work, in mothering, making meals, running errands, carpooling, imagine God himself with you in each moment. You are not alone! You might even try extending your hand out into the space next to you and considering how God might take that hand and lead you forward. Or just sit quietly with you, offering the sustenance and companionship of His Being. Right there with you.

Record your observations in a journal. Thank Him for not leaving you as an orphan but rather making His home in your heart.

Pray His Prayers. Have you ever considered that God can pray for you? When you are stuck in a moment of need, unable to even form words, instead of giving up or fearing God will float off in a more interesting direction, put on the brakes and remember Paul's words from Romans 8:26: "the Spirit helps us in our weakness."

The simplest and yet most powerful prayer can be, "Help me!"

Ask the Spirit. straight up, to pray for what you can't seem to pray. And then, wait and watch. God continuously offers His presence to assure you that you are not alone.

6

God's Provision

*"I feel lonely when it feels like my love bank
has had more taken from it than deposited
in it. Life is overwhelming and even when
I ask for help, I don't always get it."*
—Cherie

Our Struggle: I'm tired of doing everything on my own.
God's Affirmation: I will provide for you.

*A*while back, my younger brother fell ill and was hospitalized for a considerable stay in a state far away from me. His condition worsened, and the necessary medical power of attorney went into effect, appointing me to make decisions concerning his care. I spent hours on the phone with his doctors and care providers, his employer, his insurance company, his dog sitter, and his realtor since he'd just listed his home for sale and purchased a smaller place.

Oh, the decisions! Would he need extended care? What about his dogs? Should I travel in the middle of the COVID-19 pandemic to the intensely infected state where he lived? What about the move, slated for just a few weeks away? My faithful husband carried much of the emotional load with me, but he wasn't able to make the trip with me at that time.

To make matters worse, just two months prior, I'd injured my right ring finger. My young dog, Coach, had spied a bunny while I was walking him and shocked me by launching off after it, taking my finger with him. Surgery was required to repair the corkscrew dislocation and restore the tendon to a healthy position. I still wore a splint and was undergoing physical therapy. I could barely cook or type, how would I manage a move without my right hand?

My brother recovered enough to be released from the hospital but still required in-home care, so my husband and I helped him get set up in a temporary spot where he could manage until I arrived a few days later. I entered the home to find him laid out on the sofa. Within fifteen minutes it was clear to me that he could not focus on anything more than his own body. Feeding him, driving him, caring for him—and moving him—would fall to me.

The next day, two days before the move, I drove to his townhome to face what I hadn't yet absorbed: he hadn't started packing. Weeks before, his unexpected medical emergency had whisked him straight from his home to the hospital. Opening doors to discover fully stocked closets and cupboards and bending to look under beds to find undisturbed storage, I slipped over the edge of my personality's "figuring things out" bravado into "there's no way on earth I can do this" panic.

Oh, and did I mention that I was sixty-five years old at the time? My 5'3" frame was still sturdy and strong—but a move? In a city with no other family and only a few elderly-ish friends and with a bum hand?

I literally sank to my knees and begged God for help. This is too much! I can't do this!

Been there? In an overwhelmingly exhausting moment of *I'm tired of doing everything on my own*!

Physical Loneliness

Physical loneliness is a longing for skin-on help.

Likely you've heard the story of a little girl who was afraid of the dark. Night after night, she appeared at her parents' bedside for reassurance. They patiently assured her that God was with her always. "But I can't see Him!" the little girl wailed. The mom took a deep breath and responded, "I know you can't, but He's there all the same." To this, the super-honest little one confessed, "Sometimes I just need someone with skin on!"[1]

Yep, me too. We long for someone with skin on. Bones and muscles to move and lift and carry. A body to keep us warm. A mind to think things through with us. Eyes to lock with ours so we feel seen. Ears to listen so we feel heard. A hand to hold. A shoulder to nudge. A smile to share. A tear to shed. A hug to exchange.

Let's consider just how physical loneliness plagues us.

Lack of physical affection. Perhaps one of the most tangible lessons of the COVID-19 pandemic where the *world* was segregated behind doors with only immediate family members and behind masks and six feet of distance whenever venturing out in public, came the experience of deep, physical loneliness. "I miss hugs!" was the cry of grandparents, secluded in their homes, of girlfriends cut off from in-person meet-ups, of single folks forced to work remotely with no other human around.

No one to talk to. Donna has been married to Earl for a decade. A third marriage for both, they started out strong but inside their relationship, walls sprang up. Donna tried counseling. She read books. She consulted experts. Over time, Donna began to understand that Earl struggled with a deficit that imprisoned him from being able to forge authentic emotional connection. In all reality, Earl's condition won't change. So, because Donna is committed to her marriage, her need for a husband to connect with her emotions will remain unmet. She manages her need with Scripture and her vibrant faith, exercise and healthy friendships, but largely, Donna remains lonely in her most intimate relationship: her marriage.

Sex. Often, we think of physical loneliness as a longing for love. Make that the fulfilled sexual experience that expresses committed love. To hold and be held. For sure, there is that aspect to it. And more. My friend Sharon, a widow in her late forties, confesses, "I miss sex! I miss being held and cared for, and holding and caring for my husband!" Whether never-married, suddenly single, or coupled in a sex-less marriage, the physical loneliness of celibacy or just life without sex can seal us off in a bubble of pain.

Financial stress. Oh, the suffocation of finances! Where there never seems to be enough money to make even the minimum payments! So many months, a single income simply can't stretch to cover the needs of one person, much less others who depend on us. And while two-income homes might enjoy the benefit of combined resources, there are many times when even a combined amount can't stretch far enough to meet needs. The average American owes over $90,000 in debt (including credit card, student loans, personal loans and mortgages).[2] Bearing financial weight alone burdens countless ones of us with a sense of hopelessness.

Solo decision-making. To buy or rent? To move or stay put? To look for a new job? To rescue a dog or train a puppy? To invest in a kitchen remodel or save more for retirement? To put Mom in a care facility or continue to provide her care? Our minds can run in circles or veer off into ditches when considering both life-altering and everyday choices. It would be so very nice to have someone to bounce things off. We call a daughter, but she's busy with toddlers or doesn't understand the life-stage we're facing. We turn to a friend, but she's up to her ears in a project—and likely because she isn't living the solo life we are living—she concludes we have zillions of friends to tap and so dismisses our need.

No one to help. Perhaps illness strikes. We're states away from family. Or our spouse is also afflicted, and we've been the caregiver to him. We need a ride to chemo. Or help with meals. Or assistance handling the mountain of insurance forms piling up in our inbox. Or just someone to change a lightbulb in the vaulted ceiling. Overwhelmed by the overwhelming, we can be tempted simply to chuck it all. Over fifty percent of Americans (almost 125 million) are single.[3] While many more than you'd expect find their status fulfilling, a sizeable percentage struggles with the exhausting disappointment of doing life on their own when they'd expected to live in a partnership with another. Even in a stable marriage we can struggle with little help. Carol comments, "I feel lonely when I am taken advantage of by my husband, not appreciated for what I do around the house and taken for granted."

This is the summary pain of physical loneliness where we face an everyday, unending weariness in the mounting challenges and decisions and chores, without any skin-on help. So much to carry all alone!

Physical Loneliness in the Bible

Scripture offers example after example of those afflicted with physical loneliness, who expressed the loneliness of "having no one to help."

- Moses faced the impossible task of feeding the Israelites in the wilderness, crying out to God, "Where can I get meat for all these people? They keep wailing to me, 'Give us meat to eat!' I cannot carry all these people by myself; the burden is too heavy for me" (Numbers 11:13–14).
- After the confrontation with and defeat of false prophets on Mount Carmel, Elijah was overwhelmed (1 Kings 18–19). Perhaps from a spiritual exhaustion resulting from the intense battle, Elijah became afraid and ran for his life (1 Kings 19:3). He found a spot under a bush and asked God to take his life (v. 4). God strengthened him, and he traveled to Horeb where he twice cried to God, "I am the only one left, and now they are trying to kill me too" (vv. 10, 14).
- Solomon describes the difficulties of physical loneliness in his beautiful chapter 4 of Ecclesiastes.

Again I saw something meaningless under the sun:
There was a man all alone;
he had neither son nor brother.
There was no end to his toil,
yet his eyes were not content with his wealth.
"For whom am I toiling," he asked,
"and why am I depriving myself of enjoyment?"
This too is meaningless—
a miserable business! (vv. 7–8)

Examples continue in the New Testament.

- A woman lugs her jug to a well, alone, at noon to avoid the gossip and judgment of others (John 4:6–8).
- A bleeding woman reaches out to touch just the hem of Jesus's garment, so as not to make Him unclean in her pursuit of healing—a pursuit no doctor had been able to address (Mark 5:25–29).
- An invalid has "no one to help him into the pool when the water is stirred," so he remains disabled (John 5:7).
- A demoniac roams the tombs because "no one could bind him anymore, not even with a chain. . . . No one was strong enough to subdue him" (Mark 5:3–4).
- Jesus himself faced the torture of physical loneliness when tempted in the wilderness (Mark 1:12–13; Luke 4:1) and writhing in anticipation of crucifixion, with no support from the disciples (Luke 22:39–46).

Physicality and Our Faith

What does such physical neediness reveal about us as humans? Perhaps that word *need* can inform us. Need is the reality of our human condition. From Eden up until and through the cross, and even after the resurrection, we are a people of need. In order to survive, we need more than we have. And need is the doorway through which we are introduced to God, the One who provides for our need.

In nearly every expression of physical loneliness mentioned in the previous section, God's provision also appears.

- To Moses's exhaustion, God responds, "Bring me seventy of Israel's elders . . . Have them come to the tent of meeting, that they may stand there with you. I will come down and speak with you there, and I will take some of the power of the Spirit that is on you and put it on them. They will share the burden of the people with you so that you will not have to carry it alone" (Numbers 11:16–17).
- To the weary and depressed prophet, Elijah, God provides an angel to touch him and feed him—skin-on help (1 Kings 19:5)! He further provides His very presence (vv. 11–18) and finally, a successor for the lonely, heavy work in Elisha (vv. 19–21).
- In the face of the meaningless futility of solo toil, Solomon writes in Ecclesiastes 4:9–12:

Two are better than one,
because they have a good return for their labor:
If either of them falls down, one can help the other up.
But pity anyone who falls
and has no one to help them up.
Also, if two lie down together, they will keep warm.
But how can one keep warm alone?
Though one may be overpowered,
two can defend themselves.
A cord of three strands is not quickly broken.

In the New Testament, we see Jesus in the flesh, talking and listening to a scorned woman at a well (John 4:39); receiving the touch and offering healing to the unclean, bleeding woman (Mark 5:34); helping an invalid receive healing when no one else would (John 5:8–9); and restoring the demoniac to his right mind (Mark 5:15).

And in His wilderness temptation and His garden of Gethsemane torture, Jesus is ministered to by angels who attend Him (Mark 1:13) and strengthen Him (Luke 22:43).

To those suffering from the physical loneliness of "I'm so tired of doing life alone," God responds, *I will provide*. Our need reveals God's provision.

I Will Provide for You

The same day my dog ran off with my hand caught in his leash, I turned to my daily reading and discovered the exact words I would need for the days ahead. Days that would include writing a book on a keyboard (this book) and days that would also include the unexpected assignment of moving my brother: "For I am the LORD your God who takes hold of your right hand and says to you, Do not fear; I will help you" (Isaiah 41:13).

Whoa. Could words have been more perfectly fitted to my "need"? God's right hand would take my right hand. And help me.

I dug into the context, wondering if I might be making too much of such a "coincidence," and I discovered other words just earlier in the chapter, "So do not fear, for I am with you; do not be dismayed, for I am your God. I will strengthen you and help you; I will uphold you with my righteous right hand" (v. 10).

Here God was speaking to often fearful and wayward Israel, teaching them the difference between trusting in idols to help them in a time of need and trusting the care only He could provide. God gave His presence, as we've already seen. But along with His presence, He also gave His provision. Such provision comes from His "right hand," a hand that always does the righteous thing in every circumstance.[4]

I held on to Isaiah's words to Israel. That day in my brother's home, absorbing the beyond-me task before me, I sensed God nudging me to ask Him for help. Straight up help. All out help. Kinda like this: *Help!*

So, I did. I hit my knees on the cold tile of my brother's heaving home and prayed, "This is too much for me, God. *I need help—your help!*"

I sensed His simple response: *Watch for Me to provide what you need.*

So, I watched.

My first observation was in past tense. The night before as I landed at the airport, I knew I'd be responsible for packing and moving all the "small stuff," so I'd planned to rent the largest SUV I could find. Because the car rental counter closed thirty minutes before my arrival, though, I expected to have to return the next morning by taxi since my brother couldn't yet drive. To my surprise, I landed forty minutes ahead of schedule! So I wheeled my small carry-on to the counter and found it still attended. The clerk even offered me an SUV larger than the one I'd reserved—at the same price!

Hmmm. Now, on packing day number one, I began to wonder how I'd find enough containers to carry all the loads. And just what I'd use to transport them from the townhome down a long cement path to the car.

Watch for Me to provide for you.

My brother told me where to find a small trolley, how

to unlock his storage unit, and where to find the bins he'd been collecting for the move. Sliding the key in the lock and turning it to open the door, there they were. I wheeled empties to the townhome and returned them full to my car. Load after load. The car's thermometer rose with the sun's arc in the sky—registering a stunning 124 degrees at one point in the desert where I worked. (Later I'd find out it was an all-time record!) Sweat trickled down my back as the heat from the black asphalt licked my legs. I looked up for help.

A spot of shade beneath a grapefruit tree began to serve as my personal refuge in the multiple trips. Load, wheel, thank God in the shade, wheel, load into car, return the empty trolley, thank God in the shade, load again. Repeat.

When I had packed the SUV to overflowing, I drove twenty minutes to my brother's new place and began the unloading. I'd discovered that I had to unload and put away everything as best I could so I could return the empty bins to the car and head back to keep loading. I didn't have extras. But this process began to make sense to me as it meant that I was actually simultaneously moving him out and moving him in. There would be less work on the other side. And I was given respite in air conditioning between trips!

My brother had enlisted two men with a truck for the moving day. Because they had handled previous moves for him, they were familiar with his possessions and knew how he liked things managed. Armando and Armando, a father-son duo, had generous smiles, joyous attitudes and most important, strong bodies. We worked alongside each other for twelve hours to complete the gargantuan task.

The next day I faced odds and ends without Armando and Armando around to help. I needed to transition a large desk that wouldn't fit in my brother's new home to a neighbor who wanted it. However, because this neighbor was elderly, he couldn't help. I was getting the hang of this "Watch Me" posture and was able to maneuver the desk into the back of the SUV by putting one end up on the tailgate and then the other. I figured I'd be able to use gravity to lower it back to the ground—but moving it inside the other residence? No clue how that was going to happen!

As I drove the short distance, I prayed again. I need your help, God. *Watch for Me to provide for you*, came the response. I noticed a man walking his dogs, talking on his phone, a few blocks ahead. Might he help? When I opened the tailgate and used gravity to lower the desk —*Wham!*— he turned, looking over his shoulder in my direction. "Do you need some help?" he asked. *Eureka!*

I realized it was Christopher, a man I'd met previously and a friend of the neighbor receiving the desk. It also turned out that Christopher was familiar with moving furniture because his parents had run an antique store in his growing up years. Expertly, he guided me to tip the desk on end and slide it through the front door and down the hall to the waiting bedroom, where we positioned it into place. *Voila!*

I drove back to the new residence with a small load, and while I was unloading it, Manu introduced himself as my brother's next-door neighbor. "Please tell him to let me know if he needs anything? I make a mean Persian dinner!" *I see you, God!*

As I looped a load of hanging clothes over a closet rod I had recently installed, I turned with relief, realizing I'd almost transitioned his entire wardrobe. Just then, *Bam!* The rod came loose from the brackets I'd obviously installed incorrectly, sending the entire closet-full of hanging clothes to the ground in a heap. *Now what?*

I'd met one other neighbor who, I seemed to remember, had some kind of experience in construction. Since he was well into his late seventies, I hesitated to contact him. But because his name came to my mind in that very moment, I texted, "Peter, do you know anyone who might have construction experience?" He responded in seconds, "What's up?" I typed back, "Problem with a closet rod coming loose." "Can I take a look?" he queried. *You bet!* Minutes later, Peter was there, quickly diagnosing my error and proposing a solution. An hour later, the rod was reinstalled with Peter's expertise, and the clothes were back in place.

Perhaps most stunning to me of all these provisions came the next day at my brother's appointment with a medical specialist. I'd driven him to meet the doctor ninety minutes away, and at his request, I sat next to him with our combined list of questions to help us determine his next steps. Oh, how we prayed there would be hopeful next steps in the direction of healing!

The doctor entered the exam room and patiently answered all our questions while also proposing a plan. There was still hope. He would see him again in a few months. There would be no need for the drive again as it would be a telehealth appointment. *Whew.*

And then the ultimate provision. Dr. Cheng concluded his instructions and then paused with great intentionality before respectfully asking, "Would you allow me to pray over you?" My brother's surprised eyes moved from the doctor's face to mine and back and then he answered, "Of course. That would be very nice."

Dr. Cheng prayed. For healing. For hope. For our spirits to be encouraged. For God to provide for our needs. When he finished my brother lifted his head and said to Dr. Cheng, "I've never had a doctor pray for me before." *Wow.*

We drove back to my brother's new place. He sat on the couch and directed me where to place various items I didn't know how to handle, and he offered his preferences for how his bed should be made up and where paintings should be hung. A mobile notary was scheduled to arrive to sign loan documents so he wouldn't have that additional errand.

As a "big" birthday for my brother approached, I reached out to several of his local friends about surprising him a few nights later. Careful to observe COVID guidelines, I directed them to meet, in facemasks, at a specified hour on his back patio, hoping the surprise would energize and delight him. We'd just finished dinner when a line of his friends began to parade down the side of his house to his patio, one carrying a balloon, another a plant, another a gift bag, several in party hats, all singing happy birthday. *Cheers!*

Two weeks after arriving to find my brother desperately ill and unable to handle a needed move, I boarded my return flight with him "settled" in his new home. God had provided, indeed. For me. For him. For us both. In spite of my own bum hand and bent heart, God had directed me to notice my need, to ask Him for help, and to watch for Him to provide for me. And through watching, I recognized His undeniable provision.

I know, I'm sharing a story of one kind of physical loneliness, focused on the pain of having to do so much on my own. Your physical loneliness may center in another area. Physical affection. No one to talk to. The desire for sex and intimacy. Financial stress. Solo decision-making. What about these kinds of loneliness? I believe God comes as Provider in each circumstance.

To a group of weary disciples in Matthew 11:28–30, Jesus says, "Come to me, all you who are weary and burdened, and I will give you rest. Take my yoke upon you and learn from me, for I am gentle and humble in heart, and you will find rest for your souls. For my yoke is easy and my burden is light." God never intended for us to do life alone. Instead, He offers us an ongoing relationship of provision so that when we recognize our need, we can ask Him for help. And then we can watch for Him to provide for us.

PRACTICE
Watch for God to Provide

Where are you doing life all alone right now? With no one to provide help? Might you ask God for help and then watch Him provide? Might you even ask people for help and watch God provide for you through them? (Sometimes we can get stuck here; we're willing to ask God for help but drag our feet in asking others He actually might want to use to meet our needs.)

You might begin to think back over His past provisions. Fill in the blanks with at least one example of how God has brought you what you needed.

In early childhood: _____

In elementary years: _____

In middle school: _____

In teen years: _____

As a young adult: _____

In early marriage: _____

In early mothering: _____

In a work situation: _____

With friendship: _____

In a crisis: _____

During illness: _____

In a transition: _____

Now, open your heart, and your journal, in your current situation of need. Ask God for help—specifically and intentionally. Each time you notice a need, ask God to provide it. Money for groceries. Wisdom for a decision. Help with something physical.

God's Perspective

"I feel I don't fit in anywhere anymore."
—Michelle D.

Our Struggle: I feel rejected and not wanted.
God's Affirmation: I will use all things
for your good and My purposes.

When December rolls into reality, I make it a point to clear out my mailbox, the physical one, each day. We live in a complex where keyed boxes are carefully filled by a postal carrier each day. The boxes are small and in December, ours heaves with advertisements, the occasional non-autopay bill, and Christmas cards. I love them! Glittery photographed rectangles, calligraphy-addressed postcards, legit old-school cards that fold open. And the newsy letter updates.

One year though, I noticed a dread creeping into my heart as I remembered my daily errand to my mailbox. Unattended, the trepidation spread from my heart down into my soul as I turned the key and reached my gloved hand inside to grasp the daily stack. I dumped the stack on the passenger seat in my car and returned home. There, with the attitude of a robot, I slit open each envelope, glanced quickly at the photo/greeting/blah-blah-blah words, and I shuffled them back into a stack for my husband to view later in the day.

My normal eager excitement to hear from friends and families had evaporated. In its place, dry desert sand sifted in my heart, growing nothing good.

What was wrong?

I returned to the stack, grabbed my reading glasses, and curled up in my chair in front of the Christmas tree to read. "Brittany is in her third year of college now, making all A's and planning on grad school." *Good for Brittany.* "Matt and I are celebrating our fortieth wedding anniversary. We've never been more in love!" *Yippee.* "I love my job! God couldn't have placed me in a more perfect situation!" A sarcastic, sing-songy *Hmmmmm* escaped from me. "Here's a picture of our Girl Trip from last spring." *Arggghhh!* Like a green, stenchy ooze, jealousy rose up within me.

What was this about? At that time I was happily married to a great guy, we had two precious teens, and I had a fabulous but super-challenging job. I reread a few comments. I peered closer at the photos. And I realized that as I took in *their* lives, I felt a kind of "less than" about *my* life. Sizing up my life in comparison to theirs, I felt excluded from the wonderfulness others were experiencing. And as I took in the journeys of others, I felt a kind of exclusion. Why hadn't we been invited to that wedding? How come their Girl Trip didn't include me?

And then I found myself slipping down another rabbit hole. Their lives didn't seem to have the challenges my life had. Slammed doors. Missed curfews. Unmet expectations. Broken friendships. Surely, I was the only one faced with this ugly side of life.

Sometimes we feel rejected and not wanted in life. Less than. Not okay. As if we're the "only one." And that doesn't feel okay.

Situational Loneliness

When such an experience hits us hard, we can identify it as situational loneliness. This is a kind of loneliness that might be brief or might endure but is brought about by specific situations in life. Such as? Let's consider several scenarios:

Comparison. We look at the lives of others and conclude theirs are somehow "better" than ours. Far beyond the annual Christmas card updates, the continuously renewing feeds from social media with their pinteresty-perfect pictures and pithy quotes fuel our inadequacies and sequester us in the corners of our lives.

Cherie shares, "I feel lonely when I compare myself to others. I wanted to host Thanksgiving for my husband's family in our new home, but the housework was overwhelming to me. I had asked my sister-in-law for some help, and she was silent. I felt alone. I couldn't figure out how she kept her 'mansion' so clean and tidy all by herself. Until one morning I stopped over to her house to pick up a box of donated clothes. I was elated as I took in all the clutter in her house. I told her the mess made me feel so much better!"

Author Ann Voskamp writes, "There will always be people who see everything in the world as a measuring stick of their worthiness, instead of as a burning bush of God's gloriousness. If your life looks like a mess—to them—they whip out a measuring stick and feel confident of their own worthiness. If your life looks like a monument—to them—they whip out a measuring stick—and start cutting for their own empowerment."[1]

Rejection. Most of us have encountered it at least once. More likely, many times. When we're uninvited from a group we've long belonged to. When a once "safe" person is suddenly anything but. When a friend we've trusted betrays. Rejection can pull lightly on a stray thread and unravel a long-historied relationship bit by bit. Or it might slice like a knife, suddenly dealing a death blow to a relationship that had seemed to be evergreen and eternal.

One woman expresses how lonely she is "when friends go." She summarizes, "One special friend that I really connected with well seemed not to be interested or intentional about getting together the last two times I've reached out. . . . It feels like I've lost her and my heart is so sad."

Just before their annual birthday celebration, Demara's friend for forty years suddenly decided to "take a break" from their friendship, declaring Demara's family was exponentially complicated. While she understood the need to take a break for a while, Demara's heart twisted when year after year her birthday cards and even her texts went unanswered. As Lysa TerKeurst wisely observes, "Rejection steals the best of who I am by reinforcing the worst of what's been said to me."[2]

Life circumstances. Illness, parenting special needs children (sometimes just parenting period!), unemployment, divorce—it's an unending list of the situations we face that cut us off from sensing we are seen and heard by others. That we matter. That we are included.

In an unexpected moment, Jasmine was laid off from her job and finds it difficult to make her mortgage payment. She is more than concerned about health insurance. With no family to fall back on, she wonders just what to do, and she spends hours in phone queues researching options and looking for help—with little result. Never has she felt more alone!

Eryn tells of the months after her divorce when invitations to parties to which she was always invited before dried up. If she wasn't a "couple" anymore, then she wasn't included.

Michelle V. shares the story of her "neurologically diverse" adult son as he took the written test for his driver's permit, which stretched out for several hours. "During this time, he made a few friends of the DMV employees, and by the end he had a cheering section, sending smiles, prayers, and good vibes toward his success. One gentleman with whom we made a special connection asked if my son could comprehend because it seemed like he couldn't. I'm not gonna lie—comments like that still sting, and I've been fielding them for many years. Slower processing doesn't mean nonexistent processing. The gentleman graciously took in my response. But this mixed bag of joy and sorrow is always accompanied by a cloak of loneliness."

At age thirty-five, Michelle D. found herself a single mom of three. Her thirteen-year marriage crumbled, and she felt truly discarded. "Despite my best efforts to make friends, most people I interacted with just didn't know how to relate to me. And quite possibly, I didn't know how to relate to them either. All I know is I didn't feel like I fit in anywhere anymore."

The life circumstance may eventually resolve, but in the middle of the moment, loneliness looms.

Crises. Who hasn't been affected by the stunning isolation of the COVID-19 pandemic? Senior years and graduations scuttled. Weddings postponed or down-sized to immediate family only. Holidays held by zoom. No gatherings at church, in homes, around banquet tables.

In a survey of over a thousand young adults age eighteen through thirty-five, sixty-five percent reported increased loneliness, beginning with the declaration of the pandemic.[3] Struggles with mental health and substance abuse also increased.[4]

Barbara's plan to relaunch her life after retirement went sideways. "I turned sixty-five this spring and followed the Lord's leading to retire from teaching and move closer to my son and his family. One of their children is special needs, and I wanted to be able to help them. While I didn't expect them to be my only connection in this new town, the pandemic has made it impossible to plug in and get active in a church in my new town. Even meeting the neighbors is difficult."

Beyond the pandemic, issues of social justice, governmental disunity, economic downturn and unemployment, and racial strife can contribute to situational loneliness. Organizations like Meals on Wheels report that social isolation can lead to poor mental health and physical outcomes. Race-related stress can accumulate over a lifetime, leading to distrust in health providers and therefore, a decreased usage of services designed to help.[5]

Getting one's head above the falling debris of a pandemic is trying, to be sure. Add to this the issues needing to be addressed in our social world, and no wonder we struggle with a futile sense of aloneness.

Life seasons. We move from childhood to adolescence to young adulthood to mid and then later adulthood, somehow expecting that each new season will unfold with guaranteed satisfaction, on a prescribed timetable. But that doesn't always happen does it?

I can so relate to Allison's struggle as a childless woman when everyone around her was becoming pregnant. "Several years ago, many of my friends began to have children and our lives changed. All of them became mothers around the same time, and they were very busy with their babies. I had no one who could relate to what I was going through, and when I talked with my friends it was hard because they would be talking about their little ones. It was like rubbing salt into my wounded heart."

On the opposite side of things, Jessica expresses how lonely she feels as a stay-at-home mom of two very young children, "I'm home alone and a baby is crying and a toddler is screaming. Does anyone see how hard this is? Does anyone else go through this?"

Yolanda struggles to survive in the sandwich season of caring for her elderly mother while also parenting teenagers and holding down her job. She used to enjoy the respite of a girls' night or a weekend away but these days, her life is too tightly wound around meeting the needs of others to address her own. Result? She's more than lonely.

And Lee identifies that she feels "lonely when I focus on the loss of companionship with my husband, my kindred spirit. His long illness and treatments (stage four cancer) have changed his ability to relate as we did during our lives together. As I have become more caretaker than wife, and as he has had to become very dependent (so foreign to his nature), our changed roles have caused resentment and divisions that did not exist before."

This situational loneliness of being "off season" can crop up when we are single among the married, childless among parents, suddenly a mom when all our friends aren't, solo parenting kids, unemployed when everyone else is career-bound, empty-nested or not-yet-a-grandmom, or situationally the caregiver when we've been cared for in the past. Whenever our timetable runs in a sequence unlike our expectations, we can flail about wondering what happened—and lonely.

Rejected, less than, left out, spun out of control, out of sync, feeling like the only one not living their best life. Situationally lonely.

Situational Loneliness in the Bible

Where is situational loneliness seen in Scripture? Everywhere!

We need simply open our Bibles to skim the pages of Genesis to see example after example of situational loneliness.

- Adam before Eve in a situation pronounced "not good" (Genesis 2:18).
- Adam and Eve after the fall when enmity came between the man and woman (Genesis 3:16).
- Cain after comparing his portion to that of his brother, Abel, and jealously killing him, resulting in great separation from God (Genesis 4:1–16).
- Abram, Sarai, and Hagar, struggling to bear a child during a culture and time when successfully producing offspring resulted in value and being infertile diminished one's value (Genesis 16).
- Jacob stealing Esau's blessing, breaking the brothers' relationship (Genesis 26–27).
- Leah and Rachel, both married to Jacob, producing and not producing sons (Genesis 29–30).
- Joseph sold into slavery in a foreign country by his brothers and his father's devastation of his dreams (Genesis 37–50).

All these occur within just the first book of the Bible. Throughout the Old and New Testaments, the stories pile upon each other in a great car wreck of loneliness. Worn-out leaders like Moses and David. Burdened prophets like Elijah,

Isaiah, Ezekiel, Habakkuk, and Jeremiah. Barren women like Hannah and Rachel. Those who lost family and livelihood like Job, Ruth, and Naomi.

The psalmists describe various experiences of situational loneliness.

- Illness: "My friends and companions avoid me because of my wounds; my neighbors stay far away" (Psalm 38:11).
- Old Age: "Do not cast me away when I am old; do not forsake me when my strength is gone" (Psalm 71:9).
- Trials: "You have put me in the lowest pit, in the darkest depths . . . You have taken from me my closest friends and have made me repulsive to them" (Psalm 88:6, 8).

Forward it goes into the New Testament, this loneliness in so many situations. A scandalous woman at a well (John 4), a disreputable woman caught in adultery (John 8), and still another socially rejected woman subject to bleeding for over a decade (Matthew 9)—all cut off from relationship. The blind (Matthew 9), the crippled (Luke 5), the demon-possessed (Mark 1), and those infirmed with leprosy (Luke 17).

Jesus himself experienced situational loneliness.

- His own family accused Him of being "out of his mind" (Mark 3:20–35).
- He was seen as "a prophet without honor" in his own hometown (Mark 6:1–6).
- Many deserted Him at various moments in His ministry (John 6:60–71).

- He was denied three times by Peter, one of His closest disciples (Luke 22:54–62).
- His disciples abandoned Him in the garden, unable to stay awake to pray with Him (Luke 22:39–46).
- He felt abandoned by His Father while on the cross (Mark 15:34).

After Jesus's death, resurrection, and return to heaven, the disciples came to understand a very personal kind of situational loneliness of their own. The book of Acts tells of the apostles' persecution (Acts 5), Peter's imprisonments (Acts 12), Stephen's stoning (Acts 7), and then after his conversion, Paul's persecution, beatings, imprisonments, and sufferings (Acts 16, 21, 27; 2 Corinthians 11). Near the end of his life, Paul writes to his mentee, Timothy, of being deserted for his faith (2 Timothy 4:16).

The situational loneliness of rejection and not being wanted or included threads through all of Scripture.

Situations and Our Faith

As I've peeled back the layers of situational loneliness in my own life, I've come to realize that such loneliness often creeps into my being through cracks created by wrong thinking. Somehow, I swallowed a myth that in following Jesus, I could avoid struggle. Learning that "Jesus is the Answer" wooed me ahead to trust Him, yes. But I also began to view the Christian life as a formula-driven practice where my faith and efforts + Jesus's power and presence = a happy life.

Partly, this is true. Jesus's power and presence are perfect. Absolutely! The problem with this formulaic thinking is me. I'm broken. We all are. The perfect life I'd bought into is not possible here on this planet. Situations happen. And situational loneliness is the result.

In this world, there will be loneliness. Emotional. Relational. Spiritual. Vocational. Physical. Even after we address all of those aspects, there will be situations where loneliness rears its head, breathes its venomous breath, and sends fires of pain throughout our beings. We'll do better in handling the inevitable bouts of situational loneliness if we expect them and prepare ourselves with the right perspective to process them. God's perspective.

The night before He went to the cross, Jesus told His disciples, "In this world you will have trouble." But He didn't stop there. He went on, "But take heart! I have overcome the world" (John 16:33). This word *trouble* means "distress and persecution" and includes the struggle of feeling rejected and left out in situational loneliness. What Jesus said to His first-century disciples is just as true for His twenty-first-century followers. We will have trouble. But when we do have such trouble, we'll also have Jesus. When we orient ourselves to God's perspective in our loneliness, it can become survivable. Even thrive-able.

How?

I Will Use All Things for Your Good and My Purposes

The struggle with situational loneliness is a struggle with feeling rejected, left out, and not wanted. It's the experience of believing we're the only one struggling with all kinds of things no one else faces. More than other kinds of loneliness, situational loneliness results from wonky thinking. When we learn to view ourselves and the situations in our lives from God's perspective, we gain the insight necessary to cope with all situations.

God brought the lesson home to my heart one day as I was heading into a meeting and noticed a woman who seemed to me to be "all put together." She walked ahead of me into the meeting, finishing a call and then tucking her phone into her designer bag. Adorable outfit. Long and perfectly coiffed curls. Just the right amount of polish over her being. Across the table from me, I noted that when she opened her mouth to speak, she paused just a breath before making her point—an effort that gave even more wisdom to her already brilliant contribution. And before leaving, she intentionally made eye-contact with each participant around our gathering of eight, punctuating their value with her effort.

I imagined her driving home in her snazzy car, slipping into her tidy garage and holding an afternoon Bible study with her neighborhood posse before assembling a color-balanced, healthy dinner for her family. Afterward, she would put the kids down and have awesome sex with her husband.

What I would later discover—over coffee grown cold on the table between us—is that the call she took right before the meeting was her teen, confessing he'd been caught vaping at school. The day before, her husband had lost his job. And she struggled with a self-image issue, which she had to wrestle to the floor of her car before she gathered herself together to face that meeting with me. No, she didn't glide home, she crawled. And there, behind a closed and bolted door, she wept. Alone.

I learned a lesson I won't soon forget. Everybody's got something.

Every. Body.

Some. Thing.

The Dictionary of Obscure Sorrows (that's a real thing!)

defines this condition as *sonder*. Here's their complete definition: "*n*. The realization that each random passerby is living a life as vivid and complex as your own—populated with their own ambitions, friends, routines, worries and inherited craziness—an epic story that continues around you like an anthill sprawling deep underground with elaborate passageways to thousands of other lives that you'll never know existed, in which you might appear only once as an extra sipping coffee in the background, as a blur of traffic on the highway, as a lighted window at dusk."[6]

When we realize this "sonder," that everybody's got something, our perspective is shifted for good. And if we are intentional about it, our perspective is shifted for God.

We've already looked at Paul's stunning assertion in Romans 8:31–39 that there isn't *any thing* that can separate us from the love of God. God's promise that He will always love us soothes our loneliness for sure. In the verses that precede this promise, 26 through 30, Paul writes about God's perspective that can address our situational loneliness. In this section, he outlines two points that change how we cope with loneliness.

First, Paul points us to the Spirit who can pray for us when we don't know what to pray. "The Spirit helps us in our weakness. We do not know what we ought to pray for, but the Spirit himself intercedes for us through wordless groans. And he who searches our hearts knows the mind of the Spirit, because the Spirit intercedes for God's people in accordance with the will of God" (Romans 8:26–27).

A lot is packed into these two verses.

- We are not alone in our situations! The Spirit helps us in our weakness.
- We are not stuck when we don't know how to

pray in a situation! The Spirit intercedes for us
with wordless groans.

- We are not left without help in a situation! The
Spirit searches our hearts and intercedes for us with
the perfect prayer that is aligned with God's will.

I'm helped by this. Are you? Paul underlines that whatever
our situation, we are not alone in it. God shows up in His
Spirit, searches where we're stuck, and orients us to His
perspective.

Second, Paul directs us to believe that God is working
on our behalf in everything that happens to us and through
us. "And we know that in all things, God works for the good
of those who love him, who have been called according to
his purpose" (Romans 8:28).

All things. Take a minute to take that in? Every thing.
The situations where you compare yourself to others and
come up lacking. The rejections where your wounded heart
crumples and wants to crawl away. The circumstances
where you are different from others. The seasons where
you are off-sync. God says, "I will use *all* things."

Indeed, God will use *all* things.

But further, God will not just use all things for *whatever*. God will use all things for *good*. Read the verse again.
"And we know that in all things God works for the good of
those who love him, who have been called according to his
purpose." God will use all things for our good and for His
good purposes.

Admittedly, as we look at the situations in our lives, it
can be tough to see God using the less than, rejected, and
off moments in our lives for anything, much less our good
and His purposes. Even squinting, our vision remains blurry.

Sometimes it takes getting further down the road of life to get a clear glimpse of situations from God's perspective. Sometimes we're only helped to see what God sees when someone else reframes the matter and holds it up to us, someone like a counselor.

As I look back at my life, perhaps my deepest experience of rejection occurred when my father left our family. Decades later, I still cringe at the stamp of unlove that was leveled on my being at age five. That is, until God gently lifts my chin and redirects my gaze to His unending love and perspective of good. He shows me that my experience of my father's "rejection" hollowed out a spot of intense need for my heavenly Father's presence in my life. Over the years as I've healed, God has used my very wounds to help heal the wounds of countless others. To help them see their need for God as well. To help them reframe their "less-thans" to match His perspective. Yes, God has used this specific "all" for my good and His purposes.

It's an ongoing lesson.

I need to remember God's perspective. Everybody has something. And His desire is to enter into everybody's something to inhabit it—to use it and *all* things for our good and His purposes.

Embracing this reality, which is so often invisible from the outside layers of our lives, has nudged me forward with grace toward both those I know well and those I don't know at all. And perhaps even more importantly, toward myself.

In this world we WILL have trouble. Not might. Not could. Not possibly. But WILL. When we do, we will not be alone in it. Everybody has something—and SomeOne with them in it, if we want Him. SomeOne to use *all* things for our good and His purposes.

PRACTICE
Make a List of Your "All Things"

We can begin to put God's perspective into practice in our situational loneliness by first identifying our specific "situation." What's yours?

- Comparison: Are you evaluating yourself by what you see outside of you?
- Rejection: Have you experienced a rejection by someone that has left you wounded and feeling left out, uninvited, and unwanted?
- Life Circumstances: Is there a specific experience you are enduring right now that has you feeling cut off from others?
- Crises: When have you been spun out of control by an event?
- Life Seasons: Where might you be feeling out of sync in relationship to where others around you are living?

Take a look at your life and select a specific moment of situational loneliness. Now, hold that moment up to God and ask Him to give you His perspective on it.

Paul's two points from Romans 8:26–28 can help here.

First, hunker down into the reality that God doesn't leave you alone in your situational loneliness. He gives His Spirit. Bring your specific situational loneliness forward for the Spirit's help.

- You are not alone in your situation. The Spirit wants to help you in your weakness. Ask Him to help you with _____.

- You are not stuck when you don't know how to pray in a situation. The Spirit wants to intercede for you with wordless groans. Quiet yourself and allow Him to pray for _____.
- You are not left without help in a situation. The Spirit is ready to search your heart and intercede for you with the perfect prayer that is aligned with God's will. Open yourself to His examination of your heart. Then, release your _____ to Him to pray in alignment with God's best.

And second, look carefully for how you can see that God has used even this situation for your good and His purposes. What specifically has happened for good in your life because of this painful moment? How has God shaped others through you as a result of this experience?

Unlonely

God's Answer to the
Pain of Our Alone

*"If I could draw loneliness, it would be
a pale green/gray that would appear at
spots through the timeline of life."*
—Carol

It's early morning when I awaken. Slits of light appear through my bedroom shutters like slices of horizontal hope. What do I have on my calendar today, I wonder? What reason for pulling back my covers, padding over to the coffee, beginning this day? I remember my writing. This very book. How will I draw this journey through loneliness to completion? Well, certainly not completion—as I know full-well I'll never be totally free from the pain of alone and neither will you.

In my office, I sift through my files containing the stories of those friends who so generously shared when I sent out a social media plea for more perspectives than my own on loneliness. I pause over those names, praying for each one in turn. Cindy, Cherie, Lori, Carol, Julie, Ann, Joyce, Erin, Mary, Jill, Alene, Tracie, Jessica, Donna, Michelle and then another Michelle, Mitty, Nancy, Elizabeth, Bess, Cheryl, Tricia, Lyn, Kristine, Demara, Lee, Yolanda, Allison, Barbara, Jasmine, Cheryl, Karen, Tracey, Desiree, Eryn, Tracie, Nancy, Elizabeth, Lori, Laura, and others who've offered only their Insta-handle. I imagine each of them sitting at her computer, thumbing her phone, opening her heart with the "how's" of moving from lonely to unlonely. How each has not just survived but learned to thrive. A sacred journey in each precious woman, shared with me to help others.

Thank you. We all thank you.

I stack those stories on top of my own, and then I slide them into the proper categories, matching them to the various versions of loneliness. I arrange and rearrange discoveries to make them as understandable and accessible as possible for us all.

We are lonely. And God answers our "pain of alone" with himself, proclaiming over and over, "You are not alone." How do we embrace God's affirmations? How do we enter in to His solutions? How do we become "unlonely"?

Recognize and Own Your Lonely

Becoming unlonely begins when we recognize the places where we are suffering, even identifying the specific type of loneliness we are experiencing: emotional, relational, vocational, spiritual, physical, situational. When we identify our pain, we have taken the first step toward its healing.

Admittedly, this is not easy. Most of us struggle with shame around the topic, hunkering down and hiding our hard places from others and even from ourselves. And, of course, from God. But we are helped when we become honest about our feelings and take responsibility for them.

Carol shares, "Most people don't want to feel uncomfortable feelings; loneliness is one of them. Loneliness is a part of life. . . . Acknowledgement and acceptance of this feeling is important."

Julie has learned, "When I'm lonely, I'm trying to make a habit of recognizing the feelings that are coming with it. I am sad. I am not good enough. I am bored. Have I eaten? Then I can find a new perspective, pray, and find a better outlook."

Desiree has discovered that indeed, God can handle the pain of alone in her heart. "He let me scream and cry out to Him. He let me be mad. He held me in my darkest hours. He never let me go."

I'm struck by Michelle D.'s self-revelation on loneliness, "I have a pervasive feeling of anxiety that has followed me all my life. I always felt like this longing was in somebody else's hands and that there was no just no way—until I was in a relationship again—that I was going to be able to experience life without this longing and sadness and desperation. God helped me to truly understand that it is possible for us to break free of those feelings and lead us into the lives He designed for us all along." I love how Michelle realizes that instead of it being up to "somebody else," she has a role in moving to unlonely. She's not the helpless victim of loneliness but can move forward to change her life.

Yes, thank you, sisters. When I notice a moment of malaise, a morning of lethargy, a weekend of blues, or even a clingy boredom, fading in and out for weeks, I'm learning to pause and rummage about in my heart. What is this feeling? What might it be arising from? Where else have I felt it? How can I attend to it, give it light and breathe—and permission—so that I might receive what I need to learn from it?

Go to God

While recognizing and owning our loneliness comes first, and while it takes honesty and effort to recognize and own our lonely, there's more to be done. In order to move to unlonely, the next key is to go to God and, as Cherie suggests, "ask and allow Him to fill the empty spaces." In reality, it is His companionship we most desire. It is His love our hearts were created to receive. It is in relationship with Him that we enter the unending connection our beings so crave.

In his book, *Free: Rescued from Shame-Based Religion, Released into the Life-Giving Love of Jesus,* J. Kevin Butcher points out, "When we begin to own the depth of our pain, emptiness, and loneliness—and the inability of other lovers to meet the needs of our hearts—we'll find ourselves desperately longing for Jesus in a way that moves us to seek him and his love, moment by moment, like never before."[1]

Have you ever done this? Gone to God? If this thought is new to you, can I encourage you to stop for just a minute and simply pray something like, "God I need you. I know I wasn't made to do life alone but rather in relationship with you. Thank you for giving your Son, Jesus, on the cross so I can be reconciled to you as your child. Forgive me for all my waywardness. Come and be in my life, take over for me and help me to follow you and your ways." It doesn't have to be a perfect, formulaic prayer. Just tell God you want to be in a relationship with Him and ask Him to show you how. He loves you! He's waiting to hear you respond to His love.

Erin shares, "I have always believed in God, but it wasn't until recently that I have started to rely on Him, communicate with Him, and try to understand Him and His love for us. I have realized that having a relationship with God is so much more than just believing in Him. Knowing that He is always near, loving and listening and ready to comfort, makes the lonely that much less."

Once in relationship, how do we continue to go to God in everyday life? Tell Him what's going on. Ask Him to help us both understand and experience what He longs to give us: His companionship. This might come as we interact with other believers, as we worship, appreciate His creation, and pray. Often our deepest experience of God's relationship with us comes through reading His love letter to us, the Bible.

Desiree writes wise words, "Because I'm in my sixties, my life experiences have taught me to trust in God and God alone for each day of my life. Because I never know what each day will bring. . . . When you hide His words, the Bible, in your heart, they truly are a lifesaver when you can barely function. They are there in your mind and your heart, and they give you hope. They lift you up. They inspire you to go on. At first one hour at a time, then two, then three, and then a whole day."

In some seasons, our relationship with God can take a particularly tough hit, leaving us feeling abandoned and not sure where to turn. Even when we've known God for years. Cindy hit an especially rough patch during the COVID-19 pandemic. What a story she shares—helpful to all of us in those blind spots where we lose sight of God's companionship.

"When it started, I hunkered down like everyone I knew was doing. I stopped visiting my grandkids who live nearby, ordered groceries to be delivered, Zoomed my Bible study and lunch dates with friends. Our church began Zooming services. I called my friends for hour long conversations and made the most of the time connecting however I could, believing the season would be over soon.

"I'm a strong believer that God is in control and will see me through whatever comes my way. I have a rock-solid faith that has persevered through many things, but never the isolation this pandemic threw at me.

"As weeks turned into months, I began to feel myself withdrawing. I found excuses to skip my Zoom meetings and comforted myself with cooking, reading, and walking, filling up my times normally set apart to read my Bible with other things. I knew I was pulling away from people, from God. I felt rebellious and dry. And. I. Didn't. Care. Just, didn't care. I was becoming someone I didn't recognize. Instead of reaching out to other people, I began to criticize. Did you know that when you start down that track, there are *so many* things to criticize?

"I kept telling myself this was just a season of discontent. We all have those, right? I started to analyze the start of this new cycle and ask God to chip away at the hard, cold barrier that was forming around my heart. He showed me through this time that He wasn't the one who had stepped away. I knew that, but also knew that I had a choice to make. I needed to step toward Him and let Him embrace me. I confessed my waywardness, my critical spirit, my hard heart, my discontent.

"This season of loneliness has shown me that if my relationship with God is the hinge point (and it is), I have a choice to make every day, to accept what He offers me: grace, friendship, forgiveness, comfort, warmth, and delight. I can't do that on my own. I need Jesus. . . . He never stepped away. He has been there all along, just waiting for me to come back home to the full relationship He gives."

When we go to God, making Him the center from which

we have our being (see Acts 17:28), we find the most solid ground for where we belong.

Turn Outward

Once connected, or perhaps reconnected, to our Source: God and a relationship with Him through Jesus, we can continue our move toward unlonely by turning outward.

"Life is NOT about you," Desiree proclaims. "Get out of your own head and go help others. . . . You can look outside your self-pity or you can wallow in it. I have wallowed in it and only gotten more depressed. Find help, talk to a professional and help others. . . . When you reach out to others it is eye-opening. . . . Lean in, be still, hear the Father and the Son and the Holy Spirit as they love you. Then go out and share their love with others."

That's saying it, sister!

Mitty writes, "When I feel lonely, I tend to get into myself." Yup. She goes on, "However, I tend to then focus on my Bible study and thinking that others may be lonely so I write a card, an email, or a text. I think that writing a note to a friend gets me out of my thoughts." Yup again!

Tracie has learned a similar lesson. "While feeling alone, I pray for God's direction and His heart toward people. I'm more aware of others around me and as I notice them, I look for ways to be a blessing and show His love. So, I'm not focused on feeling lonely as much."

Donna "almost never" feels lonely. Why? "My default button has always been to focus on others. During the tightest lockdown of the (COVID-19) pandemic, I decided to write and send a personal card to each woman in our ministry office. There are right around forty. So each week until they returned to the office, I would carve out several hours to share a specific Scripture and note of encouragement to them. I wanted them to know someone was specifically thinking and praying for them."

Mary used the website National Day Calendar and picked one day that she thought could cheer someone else up. On National Rubber Ducky Day (January 13, by the way), she sent a short clip of Ernie from *Sesame Street* singing "Rubber Duckie" to a friend.

Oh, the relief, and even joy, that blooms when we go to God to fill us and then turn outward to allow His love to flow through us to others. Lysa TerKeurst says, "When I ease the loneliness ache in others, it is beautifully eased in me."[2] Joyce agrees, "I feel unlonely when I focus on letting God's love flow through me."

Be a Friend

Recognize and own loneliness. Go to God. Turn outward. When we keep moving in the direction of unlonely, the steps build on themselves, one after another. Here's the next suggestion: instead of asking God to provide a person for you, tell God you are willing to be a person for someone else. Be a friend.

Tracie expresses how she's actually benefitted by this process of going to God, turning outward, and then befriending others. "To combat loneliness, I have interceded and prayed for people God placed on my heart. Regardless of how I've felt, I've invited myself into the lives of others by asking them how I could pray for them, and I check in with them weekly. This opens up dialog and can even lead to lasting friendships and godly relationships. I have stopped making it about me and started putting God's agenda first."

Alene and Erin both discovered that friendship blossoms

from sharing common interests, like when they worked on something together. Groups of friends gathered around a project or a committee or planning an event or mothering concerns (such as MOPS) have grown into deep bonds that feel like family.

Jessica reports that while reduced to video meet-ups with friends, her relationships have actually deepened. She wonders if it's easier to be vulnerable somehow?

Likely, she's on to something here. While friendship often begins as we befriend others, we might not benefit ourselves unless we open ourselves to intentional risks.

As a pastor's wife, Nancy always found friendships difficult. Everyone expected her to be a friend to them without really returning the relationship. "After I bared my soul to God, He began answering my prayer. He slowly revealed to me that I was not the only one who felt alone and lonely. Other, quite confident women I knew began to express their need as I opened up my heart. Sharing my life, being vulnerable, telling my friends in a polite way . . . the truth about how I felt and asking for their help opened up a whole new opportunity for relationship connections in a deeper way. The more I practice this, the less scary it becomes. It's okay to admit when we feel alone. I've learned that people are more than ready to reach out, to love, to listen, and to offer encouragement if only I take the time, in love, to share where I am in this journey. As a result, we walk away together, each feeling encouraged, uplifted, supported, and no longer lonely."

Elizabeth, who has experienced many global moves, says, "It takes effort to beat loneliness. I've moved all around Australia and the world in my sixty-eight years. Each time I have had to put myself out there to meet 'my tribe.'" Cherie has lowered her expectations of others and embraced the reality that connection doesn't have to be in huge doses to count.

Do Something

Sometimes loneliness is soothed through the stimulation, and even distraction, of just doing something. Exercise. Volunteering. Projects. Crafts. Painting or gardening or reading. Aqua aerobics. Book clubs. Listening to music. Eating healthy. Playing online games with others. Walking on trails. Going to church. Sitting in a coffee shop, "people-watching." Teaching English as a Second Language (ESL). Cooking.

Listen to a podcast. Lori wrote to Eryn Eddy and me as a result of listening to *God Hears Her,* "My aloneness began to vanish as I felt as if you ladies were here in my apartment with me. This constant feeling of 'only I have this issue' was dispelled as I listened to you speak openly about how various things are affecting or have affected you."

But doing something also take intentionality. Desiree warns, "If you don't look for something to do, you won't find anything."

Be Grateful

Giving thanks has a way of changing the way we look at life. It actually makes us happier. There are multiple studies that reveal this finding. Robert Emmons's study divided people into three groups that each made weekly entries in journals. One group wrote five things they were grateful for. One described five daily hassles. And a control group listed five events that had impacted them in a small way. Those in the gratitude group felt better about their lives overall, were more optimistic about the future, and reported fewer health problems.[3]

Another set of studies discovered thirty-one ways gratitude can change our lives:

1. Makes us happier.
2. Makes people like us.
3. Makes us healthier.
4. Boosts our career.
5. Strengthens our emotions.
6. Develops our personalities.
7. Makes us more optimistic.
8. Reduces materialism.
9. Increases spiritualism.
10. Makes us less self-centered.
11. Increases our self-esteem.
12. Improves our sleep.
13. Keeps us away from the doctor.
14. Let's us live longer.
15. Increases our energy level.
16. Makes us more likely to exercise.
17. Helps us bounce back.
18. Makes us feel good.
19. Makes our memories happier.
20. Reduces feelings of envy.
21. Helps us relax.
22. Makes us friendlier.
23. Helps our marriages.
24. Makes us look good.
25. Helps us make friends.
26. Deepens friendships.
27. Makes us more effective managers.
28. Helps us network.
29. Increases our goal achievement.
30. Improves our decision making.
31. Increases our productivity.[4]

As a result of the study, five habits were suggested:

1. Keep a daily gratitude journal
2. Use visual reminders
3. Have a gratitude partner
4. Make a public commitment
5. Change your self-talk

Recovering from a life-altering auto accident, my niece Laura replaced the instinct to compare her life to what it used to be and instead, instituted a daily practice of gratefulness. "I want to be very careful not to put my 'prior life' on a pedestal. I want to assure my extended family and friends that I won't put their journeys on pedestals, either. I know that we all have different challenges in our lives, and it's always easier to wistfully eye someone else's journey. This is a good time for me to practice remembering all the blessings even as I endure challenges. Following my sister's wise idea, I'm going to start daily identifying and writing down something I'm thankful for that day in particular."

When we grab onto gratitude, God joins us in our everyday living in unique ways.

PRACTICE
Practice, Practice, Practice God's Six Affirmations

You are not alone. And embracing these practical steps helps us know inside and out this truth about God in our lives.

A lifestyle of "unlonely" is possible only with ongoing practice of what we believe to be true.

Identify which type of loneliness you are experiencing and work to apply God's corresponding affirmation. Review them often—along with the practice suggestion for each:

1. **Emotional Loneliness**: No one really loves me.
   God's Promise: I will always love you.
   Practice: "Inseparable" There isn't "any" thing that can separate you from God's love (Romans 8).

2. **Relational Loneliness**: No one knows the real me.
   God's Perception: I know you because I made you.
   Practice: Personalize Psalm 139.

3. **Vocational Loneliness**: My life has no meaning.
   God's Purpose: I know the plans I have for you.
   Practice: Create your own "Who Knew" list (Jeremiah 29).

4. **Spiritual Loneliness**: I feel so alone.
   God's Presence: I will be with you.
   Practice: Be present with God's presence (Matthew 28) and pray His prayers (Romans 8).

5. **Physical Loneliness**: I'm tired of doing everything on my own.
   God's Provision: I will provide for you.
   Practice: Watch for God to provide for you (Isaiah 41).

6. **Situational Loneliness**: I feel rejected, not wanted.
   God's Perspective: I will use all things for your good and My purposes.
   Practice: What's your "all" (Romans 8)?

While I've tried to remind us, it bears mentioning again, that we can weave through more than one version of loneliness at a time. Emotions and experiences don't neatly categorize themselves in our days. Rather, they spill from subject to subject, many simultaneously impacting our beings. Identifying "types" of loneliness and matching them to God's offerings is a technique to help us grab hold of what He brings to us when we most need His help.

Practicing God's affirmations in our loneliness confirms that indeed, we are not alone. In his book, *The Eternal Now*, Theologian Paul Tillich differentiates between *loneliness* and *solitude*, holding that loneliness is the pain of being alone, whereas solitude is the glory of being alone. Hard to take in, isn't it? But think about it. Loneliness, as we've been describing it, can be an endpoint if it isn't addressed with God's affirmations. Solitude is a practice that we can use to access His reminders.

Perhaps it is in our solitude that we hear God guide us out of our loneliness. It is here, at God's feet, listening to His affirmations, that we best conquer "alone" and move toward "unlonely." An unlonely that allows us to live in a new, fresh, and vibrant way.

Ahh, friend. How I pray that our journey together through the many types of loneliness and our discovery of God's many affirmations has infused you with the hope you so need today. You are not alone. May you move forward, more convinced than ever of your true Companion who walks beside you every step of the way.

A Meditation

You Are Not Alone

Are you emotionally lonely?
Do you feel like no one really loves you?
God says, *I will always love you.*

Are you relationally lonely?
Do you feel like no one knows the real you?
God says, *I know you because I made you.*

Are you vocationally lonely?
Do you feel like your life has no meaning?
God says, *I know the plans I have for you.*

Are you spiritually lonely?
Do you feel alone?
God says, *I will be with you.*

Do you feel physically lonely?
Are you tired of doing everything on your own?
God says, *I will provide for you.*

Are you situationally lonely?
Do you feel rejected, not wanted, excluded, or cut off?
God says, *I will use all things for your good and My purpose*s.

God offers:
His Promise . . .
His Perception . . .
His Purpose . . .
His Presence . . .
His Provision . . .
His Perspective.
You are not alone.

—Elisa Morgan

Notes

Chapter 1

1. Cigna US Loneliness Index, accessed April 16, 2021, cigna
.com>loneliness survey-2018-fact-sheet.

2. John Trent, "Loneliness Ends When Blessing Begins," Focus
on the Family, February 24, 2020, focusonthefamily.com/parenting
/loneliness.

3. Alexa Lardieri, "Study: Many Americans Report Feeling Lonely, Younger Generations More So," *US News & World
Report*, May 1, 2018, usnews.com/news/health-care-news/articles
/2018-05-01/study-many-americans-report-feeling-lonely-younger
-generations-more-so.

4. Christina R. Victor and Keming Yang, "The Prevalence of
Loneliness Among Adults: A Case Study of the United Kingdom,"
Jan–Apr 2012, DOI: 10.1080/00223980.2011.613875.

5. Paul Irving, "The Epidemic of Loneliness—and How to
Combat It," April 18, 2018, linkedin.com/pulse/epidemic-lone
linessand-how-combat-paul-irving.

6. Trent, "Loneliness Ends When Blessing Begins."

7. "Cigna US Loneliness Index"; Julianne Holt-Lunstad, Timothy B. Smith, et al, "Loneliness and Social Isolation as Risk Factors
for Mortality," Perspectives on Psychological Science, March 2015,
DOI: 10.1177/1745691614568352.

Chapter 2

1. Suzanne Degges-White, "The 3 Types of Loneliness
and How to Combat Them," *Psychology Today*, July 12, 2019,
psychologytoday.com/us/blog/lifetime-connections/201907/the
-3-types-loneliness-and-how-to-combat-them.

2. Gretchen Rubin, "7 Types of Loneliness, and Why It Matters," *Psychology Today*, February 27, 2017, psychologytoday.com /us/blog/the-happiness-project/201702/7-types-loneliness-and -why-it-matters.

3. Stephanie Kramer, "U.S. Has World's Highest Rate of Children Living in Single-Parent Households," Pew Research Center, FactTank, December 12, 2019, https://pewrsr.ch/2LLvbxW.

Chapter 3

1. "The Problem of Hyperindividualism and Its Impact on American Life," Wisdom WordsPPF, October 28, 2016, wisdom wordsppf.org/2016/10/28/the-problem-of-hyperindividualism -and-its-impact-on-american-life/.

2. Jean Kim, "How America Fell into Toxic Individualism," *Psychology Today*, May 25, 2020, psychologytoday.com/us/blog /culture-shrink/202005/how-america-fell-toxic-individualism.

3. "Weave: The Social Fabric Project," *The Relationalist Manifesto*, February 13, 2019, aspeninstitute.org/blog-posts/the -relationalist-manifesto/.

4. Wendy Wang, "The U.S. Divorce Rate Has Hit a 50-Year Low," Institute for Family Studies, November 10, 2020, https: //ifstudies.org/blog/the-us-divorce-rate-has-hit-a-50-year-low.

5. "The American Family Today," in Parenting in America report, Pew Research Center, December 17, 2015, pewresearch .org/social-trends/2015/12/17/1-the-american-family-today/.

6. Barna Group, email, February 15, 2021.

7. Lisa Bonos, "'You're my person': How 'Grey's Anatomy' Created a Stand-in for 'Soul Mate,'" *The Washington Post*, December 4, 2018, washingtonpost.com/lifestyle/2018/12/04/youre-my -person-how-greys-anatomy-created-stand-in-soul-mate/.

8. Marketing2Moms Survey, m2moms.com.

9. D.A. Carson, *NIV Zondervan Study Bible* (Grand Rapids, MI: Zondervan, 2015), 1173.

10. Lysa TerKeurst, *Uninvited: Living Loved When You Feel Less Than, Left Out and Lonely* (Nashville: Nelson Books, 2016), 262.

Chapter 4

1. "vocation," Lexico, lexico.com.

2. Paul Tillich, *The Courage to Be* (New Haven: Yale University Press, 1952, 2000), 47.

3. Lysa TerKeurst, *Uninvited: Living Loved When You Feel Less Than, Left Out and Lonely* (Nashville: Nelson Books, 2016), 263.

4. Os Guinness, *The Call* (Nashville: W Publishing, 1998, 2003, 2018), 59.

5. Dietrich Bonhoeffer, *Ethics* (New York: Touchstone, 1955), 253.

6. Ryan Tafilowski, "A Study on Calling: New Thoughts for an Old Idea," Denver Institute for Faith & Work, available at denverinstitute.org/a-study-on-calling/.

Chapter 5

1. TerKeurst, *Uninvited*. 259.

2. Carson, *NIV Zondervan Study Bible*, 1099.

3. J. P. Louw and E. A. Nida, (1996). Greek-English lexicon of the New Testament: based on semantic domains (electronic ed. of the 2nd edition., vol. 1, p. 464). New York: United Bible Societies.

4. Paul Tillich, *The Eternal Now* (New York, Scribner, 1963).

5. Henri Nouwen, *Reaching Out* (Garden City: Doubleday and Co., 1966), 22–23.

6. Basilea Schlink, *The Hidden Treasure in Suffering* (Lakeland: Marshall, Morgan and Scott, 1985), 35–36.

7. Sarah Young, *Jesus Calling* (Nashville: Thomas Nelson, 2004), 361.

Chapter 6

1. Vance Morgan, "Someone with Skin On," Patheos, July 8, 2015, freelancechristianity.com/someone-with-skin-on/.

2. Kim Porter, "Average American Debt," Bankrate, February 3, 2021, bankrate.com/personal-finance/debt/average-american-debt/.

3. "Singles Nation: Why Americans Are Turning Away from Marriage," WNYC Studios, September 11, 2014, wnycstudios.org/podcasts/takeaway/segments/more-half-americans-are-single.

4. Carson, *NIV Zondervan Study Bible*, 1398.

Chapter 7

1. Ann Voskamp, "A Taste of Home," *Heartlight*, November 8, 2013, heartlight.org/articles/201311/20131108_yardsticks.html.

2. TerKeurst, *Uninvited*, 81.

3. Robby Berman, "Covid-19 Has Produced 'Alarming' Increase in Loneliness," *Medical News Today*, November 25, 2020, medicalnewstoday.com/articles/alarming-covid-19-study-shows-80-of-respondents-report-significant-symptoms-of-depression.

4. Mark É. Czeisler, Rashon I. Lane, et al, "Mental Health, Substance Use, and Suicidal Ideation During the Covid-19 Pandemic," *Morbidity and Mortality Weekly Report*, CDC, August 14, 2020, cdc.gov/mmwr/volumes/69/wr/mm6932a1.htm.

5. "The Surprising Effects of Social Isolation on Mental Health in Minorities," *Partners in Nutrition Indiana, Meals on Wheels*, July 19, 2020, mealsonwheelsindy.org/the-surprising-effects-of-social-isolation-on-mental-health-in-minorities.

6. "Sonder," *The Dictionary of Obscure Sorrows*, dictionaryofobscuresorrows.com/search/sonder.

Chapter 8

1. J. Kevin Butcher, *Free: Rescued from Shame-Based Religion, Released into the Life-Giving Love of Jesus* (Chicago: NavPress/Tyndale, 2021), 5–6.

2. TerKeurst, *Uninvited*, 263.

3. Bruce Campbell, "Counting Your Blessings: How Gratitude Improves Your Health," ME/CFS & Fibromyalgia Self-Help, cfidsselfhelp.org/library/counting-your-blessings-how-gratitude-improves-your-health.

4. "31 Benefits of Gratitude: The Ultimate Science-Backed Guide," Happier Human, happierhuman.com/benefits-of-gratitude.

Want more of what you've read here?

---

elisamorgan.com

Sign up to receive Elisa's blog

Find *When We Pray Like Jesus* and more

Book Elisa to speak for your event

Listen to Elisa on the God Hears Her podcast and at discovertheword.org

---

Follow Elisa

ON FACEBOOK & INSTAGRAM,
ElisaMorganAuthor

ON TWITTER, @elisa_morgan

Elisa Morgan

Really

Living really ... Really living